Rape

Rape

Other Books of Related Interest

Opposing Viewpoints Series
Abortion
Adoption
AIDS
Child Abuse
Domestic Violence
Feminism
Human Sexuality
Male/Female Roles
Pornography
Sex
Sexual Violence
Teenage Sexuality
Violence

Current Controversies Series
The Abortion Controversy
Family Violence
Sexual Harassment

At Issue Series
Child Sexual Abuse
Date Rape
Domestic Violence
The Ethics of Abortion
Rape on Campus
Sexually Transmitted Diseases
The Spread of AIDS

Rape

Mary E. Williams, *Book Editor*

David L. Bender, *Publisher*
Bruno Leone, *Executive Editor*
Bonnie Szumski, *Editorial Director*
Stuart B. Miller, *Managing Editor*
Brenda Stalcup, *Series Editor*

Contemporary Issues
Companion

Greenhaven Press, Inc., San Diego, CA

Library of Congress Cataloging-in-Publication Data

Rape / Mary E. Williams, book editor.
    p.   cm. — (Contemporary issues companion)
  Includes bibliographical references and index.
  ISBN 0-7377-0553-1 (pbk. : alk. paper) —
ISBN 0-7377-0554-X (lib. : alk. paper)
  1. Rape. I. Williams, Mary E., 1960–   II. Series

HV6558 .R32 2001
364.15'32—dc21   00-050318
                                                           CIP

© 2001 by Greenhaven Press, Inc.
P.O. Box 289009, San Diego, CA 92198-9009

Printed in the U.S.A.

CONTENTS

FOREWORD

In the news, on the streets, and in neighborhoods, individuals are confronted with a variety of social problems. Such problems may affect people directly: A young woman may struggle with depression, suspect a friend of having bulimia, or watch a loved one battle cancer. And even the issues that do not directly affect her private life—such as religious cults, domestic violence, or legalized gambling—still impact the larger society in which she lives. Discovering and analyzing the complexities of issues that encompass communal and societal realms as well as the world of personal experience is a valuable educational goal in the modern world.

Effectively addressing social problems requires familiarity with a constantly changing stream of data. Becoming well informed about today's controversies is an intricate process that often involves reading myriad primary and secondary sources, analyzing political debates, weighing various experts' opinions—even listening to firsthand accounts of those directly affected by the issue. For students and general observers, this can be a daunting task because of the sheer volume of information available in books, periodicals, on the evening news, and on the Internet. Researching the consequences of legalized gambling, for example, might entail sifting through congressional testimony on gambling's societal effects, examining private studies on Indian gaming, perusing numerous websites devoted to Internet betting, and reading essays written by lottery winners as well as interviews with recovering compulsive gamblers. Obtaining valuable information can be time-consuming—since it often requires researchers to pore over numerous documents and commentaries before discovering a source relevant to their particular investigation.

Greenhaven's Contemporary Issues Companion series seeks to assist this process of research by providing readers with useful and pertinent information about today's complex issues. Each volume in this anthology series focuses on a topic of current interest, presenting informative and thought-provoking selections written from a wide variety of viewpoints. The readings selected by the editors include such diverse sources as personal accounts and case studies, pertinent factual and statistical articles, and relevant commentaries and overviews. This diversity of sources and views, found in every Contemporary Issues Companion, offers readers a broad perspective in one convenient volume.

In addition, each title in the Contemporary Issues Companion series is designed especially for young adults. The selections included in every volume are chosen for their accessibility and are expertly edited in consideration of both the reading and comprehension levels of the audience. The structure of the anthologies also enhances accessibility. An introductory essay places each issue in context and provides helpful facts such as historical background or current statistics and legislation that pertain to the topic. The chapters that follow organize the material and focus on specific aspects of the book's topic. Every essay is introduced by a brief summary of its main points and biographical information about the author. These summaries aid in comprehension and can also serve to direct readers to material of immediate interest and need. Finally, a comprehensive index allows readers to efficiently scan and locate content.

The Contemporary Issues Companion series is an ideal launching point for research on a particular topic. Each anthology in the series is composed of readings taken from an extensive gamut of resources, including periodicals, newspapers, books, government documents, the publications of private and public organizations, and Internet websites. In these volumes, readers will find factual support suitable for use in reports, debates, speeches, and research papers. The anthologies also facilitate further research, featuring a book and periodical bibliography and a list of organizations to contact for additional information.

A perfect resource for both students and the general reader, Greenhaven's Contemporary Issues Companion series is sure to be a valued source of current, readable information on social problems that interest young adults. It is the editors' hope that readers will find the Contemporary Issues Companion series useful as a starting point to formulate their own opinions about and answers to the complex issues of the present day.

INTRODUCTION

A look at the edicts of the ancient world reveals that rape is an age-old crime that often merited severe punishment. Ancient Normans would cut off a rapist's testicles and gouge out his eyes. The laws of Rome and Saxony demanded the execution of rapists, and Hebrew law required that rapists be stoned to death. Ancient Hindus also sentenced rapists to death and believed that their souls would never be pardoned.

However, not all societies punished rapists so harshly. Many cultures, in fact, defined rape in relation to marriage. In ancient Assyria, for example, the rape of a virgin was considered to be an infraction against her father: An unmarried woman's virginity was highly valued, and rape therefore lowered the amount of the bride price that her father could command from her prospective husband. In compensation, the father and brothers of an unmarried rape victim were granted permission to rape the women in the rapist's family. Other societies allowed a practice known as "bride capture," in which a man could lay claim to a woman as his wife by kidnapping and raping her. In her often-cited 1975 book *Against Our Will: Men, Women, and Rape*, feminist writer Susan Brownmiller asserts that for many cultures marriage "appears to have been institutionalized by the male's forcible abduction and rape of the female. . . . Forcible seizure was a perfectly acceptable way—to men—of acquiring women, and it existed in England as late as the fifteenth century."

These insights about the historical connection between rape, male ownership of women, and marriage have influenced contemporary theories about the causes of rape. Some researchers argue that rape is an inevitable result of a patriarchal, or male-ruled, society. In such societies, men are generally expected to be aggressive and dominant, while women are expected to be passive and deferential. Though women today may no longer be considered the property of their fathers or husbands, overall their political, economic, and social status is secondary to that of men, and an imbalance of power continues to exist between the sexes. Rape is one means by which men as a group perpetuate their domination over women, many feminists and social scientists contend. They maintain that although most men are not rapists, all men profit from the fact that some men rape. As feminist essayist Susan Griffin writes, "The existence of rape in any form is beneficial to the ruling class of [males]. For rape is a kind of terrorism which severely limits the freedom of women and makes women dependent on men."

This hypothesis that rape is a violent form of male social dominance is often referred to as the sociocultural theory on rape. Since the 1970s, the sociocultural assertion that "rape is a crime of violence, not sex" has been the predominant view concerning rapist motivation. Proponents of this theory contend that rapists are provoked not by sexual desire but by hostility toward women and a need to control their victims. Sex is simply the means by which rapists exert violent aggression, argues Susan Brownmiller: "[Rape] is not a crime of lust but of violence and power. . . . Rape victims are not only the 'lovely young blondes' of newspaper headlines—rapists strike children, the aged, the homely—all women."

The sociocultural theory on rape is often cited to explain not only rape committed by strangers but also rape committed by a person the victim knows. In examining the causes of "date" or acquaintance rape, researchers point to social factors that they claim are commonly found in patriarchal cultures, such as the persistent conditioning of males to be tough and competitive and the belief that one must be aggressive to be masculine. Some men are also taught from an early age that the use of force or violence is an acceptable way to solve problems. "Such males are likely to be more controlling and aggressive toward women," states Peggy Reeves Sanday, author of *A Woman Scorned*. When these men become involved in a romantic or dating relationship, Sanday points out, sex may become "one of the arenas where dominance and control are acted out," resulting in rape. Date rapists may also buy into the popular notion that their masculinity is defined by the amount of sexual activity they engage in. "Males who look to sexual conquest for self-esteem are more likely to force girls into sexual acts," Sanday contends.

While the sociocultural theory is currently the prevailing view on the cause of rape, it is not the only theory about rapist motivation. A number of researchers believe that biological factors and mental illness provoke certain men to be sexually violent. Paraphiliac disorders, for instance, are illnesses that can cause people to compulsively and repeatedly commit sexual abuse. Such disorders may be the root cause of several kinds of sexual offenses, including child molestation, serial rape, and sexual homicide, some criminologists maintain. Men suffering from paraphiliac disorders often claim that they are plagued by repetitive urges and violent fantasies involving rape, sexual sadism, and murder. Though these men may attempt to suppress their violent thoughts, they eventually reach a "breaking point" that triggers an episode of sexual brutality.

In an attempt to rehabilitate convicted sex criminals and prevent repeat offenses, some states have authorized the use of Depo-Provera and Depo-Lupron, drugs that lower the body's production of the male sex hormone testosterone. Proponents maintain that injections of Depo-Provera, a practice also known as "chemical castration," can effectively curtail many paraphiliac disorders. One Maryland rapist who received Depo-Provera injections during and after his incarceration insists that his treatment has been successful: "The will to have sex [is] still there. . . . But Depo-Provera allows you the time, mentally, to make the decision about whether this is an appropriate behavior. . . . Sex doesn't control me anymore."

Critics caution, however, that Depo-Provera is effective for only a subset of rapists, and they warn against drawing the conclusion that rape is always caused by testosterone-related sexual disorders. In fact, some criminologists argue that a confluence of biological, psychological, and social factors induces men to rape. According to these experts, an individual who has a genetic propensity to aggression and also suffers childhood neglect or abuse may develop a withdrawn and violence-prone personality. Placed in a social environment that conditions men to be dominant and sexually aggressive, this maladjusted individual may easily become a rapist. Serial rapist and murderer Ted Bundy, for example, apparently experienced parental neglect and bullying from classmates when he was a child. Before his execution in 1989, Bundy claimed that his exposure to hard-core pornography during adolescence influenced his later crimes. As viewed by the confluence theory, Bundy's early experiences—perhaps combined with genetic or biological factors—increased the chances that he would eventually become a violent sex offender.

Still another theory on why some men rape involves scientific speculation about male biology and evolution. Challenging the sociocultural theory that "rape is an act of violence, not sex," evolutionary biologist Randy Thornhill and anthropologist Craig T. Palmer contend that rape is indeed a sexually motivated crime. Furthermore, they argue that the causes of rape are firmly rooted in the process of human evolutionary adaptation. According to Thornhill and Palmer, men are biologically wired to ensure the continuation of the species by impregnating as many women as possible. Women, on the other hand, possess a biological tendency to select healthy male partners who are good providers—a "choosiness" that increases the chances that their offspring will be healthy and survive into adulthood. Rape, then, "arises from men's evolved machinery for obtaining a high number of mates in an environment where females choose mates," the two scientists assert. Supporting this hypothesis that rape is connected to the reproductive drive, Thornhill adds, are statistics revealing that the majority of rape victims are young women of childbearing age. Thornhill and Palmer stress that the evolutionary explanation is not meant to excuse or justify rape, and they believe that a wider acceptance of this theory could help societies develop more successful approaches to reducing and preventing rape.

Nevertheless, many feminists and social scientists take issue with the evolutionists' theory. They charge that this hypothesis does not provide an adequate explanation for the devastating physical and psychological trauma that can accompany rape. Such violence and trauma do not seem to have any evolutionary purpose, maintains feminist critic Barbara Ehrenreich: "We are . . . talking about appalling levels of damage to the mother of the rapist's prospective offspring. Most rape victims suffer long-term emotional consequences—like depression and memory loss—that are hardly conducive to successful motherhood." Evolutionary scientists, however, counter that the social science view on rape completely neglects possible biological influences on behavior, relying too much on fashionable and "politically correct" notions about environmental and cultural factors. Author Wendy McElroy, herself a victim of rape, agrees that the socio-cultural view is too limited: "We need a theory [about rape] that explores the complexity of the issue, not one that oversimplifies it for the sake of a political agenda."

Scientists, researchers, and criminologists have come to no single conclusion about the causes of rape, yet they all agree that the problem of sexual violence demands persistent attention and investigation. Statistics on crime reveal that while the rates of murder, robbery, and assault have decreased in recent years, the number of reported rapes has not declined and has actually increased in some regions. Experts hope that uncovering the motivation for rape will help reverse this disturbing trend. The various theories on the causes of sexual assault are presented and explored in *Rape: Contemporary Issues Companion*. The authors also examine the legal quandaries that can arise in rape cases, the effects of sexual violence on its victims, and various methods for reducing and preventing rape.

CHAPTER 1

RAPE AND SEXUAL ASSAULT: AN OVERVIEW

Contemporary Issues
Companion

RAPE AND ITS EFFECTS ON VICTIMS

Bonita Repp

Rape is a crime of sexual violence that causes long-term emotional devastation in its victims, contends Bonita Repp in the following selection. Victims come from all walks of life, she points out, and most are acquainted with their attackers. Although rape can occur anywhere, Repp writes, it is largely underreported because many victims do not want to face the painful medical and legal processes that force them to relive the attack. Moreover, the author maintains, many communities and courts of justice subscribe to the myth that victims are in some way to blame for their sexual assault. If victims did not have to face such stigmas, the battle against rape would become more successful, she concludes. Repp is an advocate for the Women's Coalition of St. Croix, Virgin Islands, an organization that provides social services to victims of rape and domestic violence.

We have all read about the extremely high incidence of rape being committed in our community. These crimes are a highly traumatic, personal violation of the victim and the victim experiences a wide gamut of fear, anger, guilt and shame.

Because of the societal stigma, the painful hospital exam, the humiliating legal procedures, which include hours and hours of telling and retelling, living and reliving the rape, the personal attacks on an adult victim's character in the courtroom (and recently in the newspapers), it is estimated that as high as 90% of rapes go unreported.

There tend to be myths about rape which people believe to be fact, particularly in cases where the victim knows the perpetrator(s). Society has created these myths in order to feel safe. "If I don't wear this, if I don't do that, if I don't go there, I will not be raped." The fact is that *anyone* can be sexually assaulted.

Victims range in age from infants to people in their nineties. Victims are male or female from every racial, ethnic, religious, economic and social background.

Victims are attacked in their homes, working in offices or stores, walking to or from their cars, waiting for or exiting buses, out on dates, hanging out with trusted friends, walking to or from school, *any* situation where a predator can take advantage.

Statistics show that 84% of all sexual assaults are committed by an acquaintance of the victim, 57% of all sexual assaults occur during a date, and 43% of all rapes involve two or more perpetrators.

Problems Victims Face

Even though rape is the most under-reported crime due to all the fear, pain and humiliation the victim suffers, first at the hands of the rapist, then at the hands of the justice system, many people believe that women frequently "cry rape." The FBI reports that false accusations account for only 2% of *all* reported sexual assaults, which is no higher than false reports for any other crime.

People also seem to believe strongly that without some cooperation from the victim, there can be no rape. The fact is that rapists are willing to use all the force necessary to accomplish penetration. Many victims do not resist because they fear for their lives. Submission to save your life or avoid bodily harm is not the same as cooperation.

Afterwards victims are often most disturbed by the terror they experienced and re-experience as being completely vulnerable. They know that during the rape, the rapist had the power to do anything to them, including take their lives. And there are no guarantees. Some women have been brutalized even though they submitted. There are no rules on how to survive a sexual assault.

The Dynamics of Rape

Some people believe that rape results from an uncontrollable sexual urge, that men rape impulsively and out of biological need. Rape is a criminal act of violence using sex as a weapon. Men rape to express hostility and to dominate. They rape because it allows them to express anger and to feel powerful by controlling another person.

Studies show that most rapes—including acquaintance rape—are planned hours or even days in advance. Additionally, most convicted rapists are married or have available sex partners, which supports rape being a learned, planned behavior that does not arise from impulsive biological need.

Many people, men in particular, do not understand the dynamics of rape. If you have any doubt, just ask a few men when was the last time they had fears of being raped and how they would feel if they were raped. Most immediately think of a woman seducing them against their will, and the depth of violation known to rape victims does not even enter their minds. This is because rape is almost exclusively a male crime.

It is the male who penetrates, who violates by thrusting part of his body *into* the woman's, man's or child's body. The only way a female can perform the act of rape is to penetrate with an object.

Rape is the act of someone penetrating your person without your consent. This act and other acts of sexual abuse and sexual assault have devastating, long-term emotional, psychological and, in the case of children, developmental consequences to the victims. That is why it is so important for victims to be heard and believed and supported through the ordeal of the legal process, if they choose to report, and during the long recovery process so that they are able to reclaim their lives.

Why Rape Is Underreported

No one asks to be raped, but it is easy to understand why a victim might choose not to report a rape. The medical exam is painful and the legal process forces the victim to visit and revisit the rape. Then, especially in cases where the victim knows the perpetrator, there is always a fear with regards to the victim's safety and the victim can count on being degraded and humiliated in court by the defense attorney. Does this sound like something you would choose to experience?

Why is it that we as a society question the validity of violent crimes committed against women and children? The victims of other criminal acts are not scrutinized and placed on trial right along with the defendants, or just totally ignored by the community and the justice system.

Perhaps if we as a society were to take the stigma away from the victims and place the blame and responsibility soundly on the perpetrators, more victims would feel safe to come forward and eventually we would have fewer crimes of this nature. It is our own complacence which allows these predators to roam freely among us, doing as they please, because it is so much easier for us to hide in the myths and blame the victims.

Exaggerated Rape Statistics Cause Unnecessary Alarm

Linda Seebach

One of the most commonly reported national statistics on sexual assault is that one out of four women has experienced rape or attempted rape. In the following selection, editorial writer Linda Seebach questions the validity of similar statistics that resulted from a survey conducted by the Colorado Coalition Against Sexual Assault. According to Seebach, the surveyors used an overly broad definition of rape that did not take into account whether the respondents expressed lack of consent or whether they considered themselves to be rape victims. This overgeneralized definition of rape, Seebach concludes, has led to exaggerated and sensationalized reporting on the incidence of rape.

Colorado's rape survey invited banner headlines—and got them. "1 in 7 women raped," said the *Denver Rocky Mountain News*, and that was a restrained interpretation compared with the official press release, which claimed the survey "revealed that 1 in 4 women and 1 in 17 men have been raped."

But the results are much more ambiguous than that, and the headlines are dangerously misleading.

The survey was carried out by Colorado Sexual Assault Prevention, a program of the state Department of Public Health and Environment and the Colorado Coalition Against Sexual Assault. They added their questions about assault to an ongoing statewide telephone survey about health and health-related behavior. To interpret the results, you have to know how the questions were asked. The interviewer defined sex for the respondents as any type of penetration or intercourse, and then asked "Has anyone ever had sex with you against your will or without your consent? This would include situations where verbal threats, coercion, physical force or a weapon was used or you were not able to give consent for some reason." Next the interviewer asked respondents whether anyone had ever attempted to have sex with them against their will, and third whether either had happened in the past 12 months.

The questions approximate the legal definition of sexual assault, but do not use the terms "sexual assault" or "rape"—intentionally, the

Reprinted from Linda Seebach, "Rape Report Causes Unnecessary Alarm," *Denver Rocky Mountain News*, August 8, 1999. Reprinted with permission from the Denver Rocky Mountain News.

survey report says, because "respondents might not associate their experiences with these terms."

I sympathize with the reason for framing the questions this way; it's to counter the view, less prevalent now than it once was, that rape is something that occurs only between strangers. The guy who jumps out of the bushes or invades the bedroom is a rapist, but never a husband who forces sex on his wife or a boyfriend who insists on sex when both he and the woman are too muddled by alcohol or drugs to know whether there is consent.

Scary and Misleading Statistics

The former prejudice is wrong. But applying the term "rape" to every ambiguous encounter, regardless of the outcome or what the people involved would call it, is equally extreme, and that's the only way to arrive at a scary statistic like "1 in 4."

Of the 948 women in the survey who answered these questions, 704, or 74 percent, had no history of sexual assault; 96, or 10 percent, said they had experienced what the survey defined as an attempted assault; and 148, or 16 percent, said the assault was completed. The researchers didn't ask how many of them knew their assailant, but national surveys suggest the figure is usually around 80 percent.

Among men, 47 of 784 had experienced an attempted or completed assault by the survey's definition. During 1998, it was seven women and one man.

Of course that's too many, but does it mean that people, especially women, should plan their every activity around fear of rape? Not to me, but I worry that will be the effect of overgeneralizing the term. Reasonable prudence, especially in the choice of one's friends, is appropriate, but not abject terror.

I worry, too, that the exaggerated claims are unfair to men. Even if a quarter of women have had an inappropriate sexual experience some time in their lives, that does not imply that a quarter of men are to blame. "Men have to learn," one person involved in the study told me, "that this is not acceptable behavior."

But most men already know that. There are serial jerks as well as serial rapists, and if three-quarters of adult women have successfully avoided all of them for a lifetime, they must be fairly rare.

The survey estimates that 11,440 sexual assaults took place in Colorado in 1998, a number it derives by extrapolating the eight incidents researchers found to the entire adult population of the state. Only a sixth as many, about 1,800, were reported to law enforcement. Is that because sexual assault is "one of the most underreported crimes in this country," as the report suggests, or is it because many of these incidents really are not criminal? From eight cases, it is impossible to tell.

This is the first statewide survey of its kind. If it' s repeated, I hope the results are presented in a less sensational manner.

DEFINING AND STUDYING ACQUAINTANCE RAPE

Peggy Reeves Sanday

Peggy Reeves Sanday is the author of *A Woman Scorned: Acquaintance Rape on Trial*, from which the following selection is excerpted. Sanday traces acquaintance rape research from its beginnings in the 1970s to the recent investigations of the late 1980s and early 1990s. She discusses the often-cited studies of Susan Brownmiller, Diana Russell, and Mary Koss, the feminist researchers who have claimed that the majority of rapes are committed by men known to the victims. Subsequent research has revealed that women report acquaintance rape far less often than rape committed by strangers, writes Sanday, and that drugs and alcohol are often factors in acquaintance rape. Several studies conclude, moreover, that acquaintance rape victims may not recognize their assaults as rape—many women do not define coerced sex as rape unless the attacker is a violent stranger, Sanday points out.

Martha McCluskey went to college during a time when feminist activism for rape reform was well under way, however not yet widely publicized outside scholarly and legal circles. In 1977 she was sexually abused by a group of fraternity brothers while a student at Colby College. At the time, however, Martha thought that being assaulted by "normal white college men . . . was not significant" and she didn't understand it as "real violence." It wasn't until after graduating from Yale Law School that she wrote about the assault in an article in the *Maine Law Review* on "privileged violence in college fraternities."

It happened at the beginning of vacation, when her dorm was nearly empty. As she described it:

> I am standing in the hallway looking out the window for my ride home. I turn around and my suitcase is gone; Joe and Bill from down the hall are laughing as they carry it away. I follow them. I hear a door lock behind me. They let go of my suitcase and grab me.

I am lying on the bare linoleum floor of Joe's bedroom. In the room are a group of Lambda Chi and KDR pledges who live on my hall; several of them are football players. Some are sitting on the bed, laughing. Two others are pinning my arms and my legs to the floor. Joe is touching me while the others cheer.

I am a friendly fellow-classmate as I reasonably explain that I'm in a rush to catch a ride, that I'm not in the mood to joke around; that I'd really like them to please cut it out. It takes a few long upside-down seconds before things look different. As I start to scream and fight I feel like I am shattering a world that will not get put back together. They let me go.

Later I don't talk about this, not even to myself. I sit near Joe and Bill in sociology and English classes. I don't talk in class.

Early Research on Acquaintance Rape

Starting in the 1970s, research on acquaintance rape conducted by psychologists, sociologists, and medical researchers began, and by the 1990s a significant body of knowledge on all aspects of sexual assault and abuse had been established. At first the research focused on the annual incidence and lifetime prevalence of acquaintance rape in order to establish the scope of the problem, but soon expanded to include causes, consequences, social and psychological costs, and prevention. The studies operated within the legal definition of rape as sexual intercourse, including oral or anal penetration, due to force, the threat of force, or by taking advantage of a person's incapacity to consent. Most studies focused on the heterosexual rape of females. However, in recent years attention has turned also to the heterosexual and same-sex rape of male victims. Least attention has been given to same-sex rape of women.

Studies making a distinction between jump-from-the-bushes stranger rape and rape involving people who know one another go back at least to the 1950s. In 1952 the *Yale Law Journal* recognized that rape ranges from "brutal attacks familiar to tabloid readers to half won arguments of couples in parked cars." Harry Kalven and Hans Zeisel's distinction between "aggravated" and "simple" rape in their national study of fifties trials was the first to demonstrate that a significant proportion (40 percent) of rape cases going to trial involved acquaintances. Both of these acknowledged that when the parties know one another a conviction is much more difficult. Kalven and Zeisel were able to attribute the difficulty to juror prejudice by showing that judges were much more likely than jurors to believe that the evidence warranted a conviction in cases of simple rape.

The most well-known of the early studies acknowledging the scope of acquaintance rape was authored by sociologist Menachem Amir.

Based on an examination of police files of rapes occurring in 1958 and 1960, Amir concluded that rapists are generally "normal" men. About half of all the rapes were committed by men who knew their victims. Only 42 percent of the rapists were complete strangers to their victims, and not all of the victims resisted to the utmost. More than half of the victims were submissive during the rape; about one fifth of the victims put up a strong physical fight; and another quarter actively resisted in some other way, like screaming. Twenty percent of the victims were between the ages of ten and fourteen, and 25 percent between fifteen and nineteen. The younger the victim the less likely she was to resist.

Susan Brownmiller

The first widely read feminist studies mentioning acquaintance or date rape were authored by Susan Brownmiller and Diana Russell in the mid-1970s. In her landmark study, *Against Our Will,* Brownmiller is the first to use the term "date rape." The kind of interaction Brownmiller labeled date rape was typical of men and women caught in the double bind of the sexual revolution. Men pressed their advantage thinking that all women now "wanted it," but nice girls hadn't yet learned to make a no stick. Brownmiller phrased the problem as follows:

> In a dating situation an aggressor may press his advantage to the point where pleasantness quickly turns to unpleasantness and more than the woman bargained for, yet social propriety and the strictures of conventional female behavior that dictate politeness and femininity demand that the female gracefully endure, or wriggle away if she can, but a direct confrontation falls outside of the behavioral norms. These are the cases about which the police are wont to say, "She changed her mind afterward," with no recognition that it was only afterward that she dared pull herself together and face up to the fact that she had truly been raped.

Brownmiller's historic contribution to the anti-rape movement is in her valuable analysis of the cultural forces shaping female passivity when confronted with male sexual aggression and her conceptualization of rape as violence. Brownmiller urged a generation of young women to learn to say no and overcome their historical training to be nice. She recognized that date rapes hardly ever get to court and don't look good on paper because the "intangibles of victim behavior . . . present a poor case." These are the kinds of cases that Kalven and Zeisel found usually ended in acquittals. Brownmiller admits that even with her feminist awareness she often feels like shouting, "Idiot, why didn't you see the warning signs earlier?" upon hearing such cases.

Diana Russell

Before she began researching rape in the early 1970s, Diana Russell held the "crazed stranger" theory of rape, believing that rape was "an extremely sadistic and deviant act, which could be performed only by crazy or psychopathic people." The idea had never occurred to her that rape by a lover, friend, or colleague was possible. She learned differently in 1971 while she was attending the highly publicized rape trial of Jerry Plotkin in San Francisco. Plotkin was a jeweler accused of abducting a young woman at gunpoint to his swank apartment, where he and three other men raped and forced her to commit various sexual acts.

During the trial, which drew many feminist protestors, Russell began hearing stories from other women who had been raped but who had not reported the rape, fearing the treatment they would probably receive in the courtroom. The outcome of the Plotkin trial was a grim reminder of why so few were willing to report. The jury acquitted Plotkin because of the complainant's prior sex life, which was gone over in minute detail in the courtroom. Convinced of the injustice of the verdict and aware of the need for further education, Russell embarked on a program of research that would produce two of the most important early studies of acquaintance rape.

Russell's first book, *The Politics of Rape*, was based on interviews with ninety women. In chapters titled "Lovers Rape, Too," "Some of Our Best Friends Are Rapists," and "Fathers, Husbands, and Other Rapists," to name just a few, Russell records women's experiences which demonstrate that rape is just as likely to occur between acquaintances as between strangers. The level of force employed during rape ranged from intimidation in some instances to extreme force in others. A typical case is reflected in one woman's statement that she put up as much struggle as she could, but he "used all of his strength, and he was very forceful and kept [her] down." Another woman, who was raped by a fraternity brother, said she didn't scream because she was afraid he would call his frat brothers and "run a train" on her.

The reasons these women gave for not reporting their experiences reflect the dominant belief that to do so would be embarrassing and useless. The first woman thought about going to the police but decided against it, believing that her accusation of rape would be impossible to prove. The woman who was raped by the frat brother told a close friend but remained silent otherwise, due to depression. Another woman, who had been gang raped after getting into a car, told her brother, who called her a whore. When she told her husband many years later, he started punching her in the head. She never thought of going to the police, for fear of how her parents would react. One by one the women Russell interviewed gave similar reasons for not reporting.

In 1978, Russell conducted a survey in San Francisco of 930 randomly selected women ranging in age from eighteen to eighty. Her results provided a statistical profile of acquaintance-versus-stranger rape in a diverse population of all social classes and racial/ethnic groups. The study followed the legal definition of rape in California and most other states at that time. Questions were asked about experiences of forced, nonconsensual intercourse as well as about experiences of "unwanted" sexual intercourse while asleep, unconscious, drugged, or otherwise helpless. The inclusion of the question about physical helplessness due to alcohol or drugs also was in keeping with the legal definition of rape in California. Russell was very careful to exclude from the rape category any experiences in which women reported *feeling* rather than *being* forced.

Of the 930 women, 24 percent reported at least one completed rape, and 31 percent reported at least one attempted rape. Russell used the term acquaintance rape as an umbrella term to distinguish rapes involving people who know one another from rapes involving strangers. Thirty-five percent of the women in her study experienced rape or attempted rape by an acquaintance (ranging in degrees of intimacy from casual acquaintances to lovers) as compared with 11 percent raped by strangers and 3 percent by relatives (other than husbands or ex-husbands.) Only 8 percent of all incidents of rape and attempted rape were reported to the police. These incidents were much more likely to involve strangers than men known to the victim.

Mary Koss

Another important early survey was conducted in 1978 by psychologist Mary Koss of nearly four thousand college students at Kent State University, where she taught. As a young psychology professor just starting out in the mid-seventies, Koss had read Susan Brownmiller's book on rape and felt that the next step should be a scientific study of the epidemiology of rape. When she first designed the Kent State study, Koss preferred the label "hidden rape" to "acquaintance rape" because of the growing recognition in law enforcement circles that rape was "the most underreported of major crimes." She chose to study "unacknowledged victims of rape," women who have experienced forced sexual intercourse but do not call it rape.

In criminology terms, the unacknowledged victim is the "safe victim." For law enforcement purposes it is always important to identify the kinds of people most likely to be safe victims in any class of crime so that they can be protected through educational programs informing them of their rights. At the time Koss embarked on the Kent State survey, government estimates suggested that "only 40–50 percent of the rapes that occur each year are reported to the police."

Koss's goal was to determine the prevalence of hidden rape. For the survey, she identified four degrees of sexual aggression ranging from what she called "low sexual victimization" to "high sexual victimization" in order to separate gradations of sexual abuse. The category labeled "high sexual victimization" was the category that Koss defined as rape. It included women who said they had experienced unwanted intercourse or penetration of the mouth or anus from a man or men who used or threatened to use physical force. Koss separated this category of rape victims into two types: women who acknowledged they had been raped and those who did not name what happened to them as rape. Koss found that 13 percent of the women interviewed answered yes to at least one of three questions asking them whether they had experienced forced penetration at any time since the age of fourteen. Only 6 percent of the women interviewed, however, answered yes to the question "Have you ever been raped?"

Less than 5 percent of the men in the study admitted to using force. Those who admitted to using force were remarkably similar to the sexually aggressive men described in Lester Kirkendall's 1961 study of 1950s college men. For example, like their 1950s counterparts, the Kent State males expressed attitudes illustrative of the double standard. They were more approving of sexual relationships with prostitutes and more disapproving of sexual freedom for women than the less aggressive men in the study. They preferred traditional women, who were dependent, attention-seeking, and suggestible. Their first experiences with sexual intercourse tended to be unsatisfactory, but they expressed more pride in these experiences than the less aggressive men. When asked if they had sex the first time because it was socially expected, nearly half of the men in the sexually aggressive groups answered yes, as compared with only a quarter of the nonsexually aggressive men.

There were other differences between the types of men in Koss's study reminiscent of Kirkendall's findings. The highly sexually aggressive men were more likely to identify with a male peer culture. More were likely to be in fraternities than those reporting no or low sexual aggression. They were more insensitive to the woman's resistance and more likely to think that sexual aggression was normal sexual behavior, part of the game that had to be played with women. They believed that a woman would be only moderately offended if a man forced his way into her house after a date or forced his attentions in other ways.

Recent Studies

To see whether she could replicate her Kent State findings in a nationwide sample, Koss joined with *Ms.* magazine in a 1985 survey of 6,159 students on thirty-two college campuses. The results of this survey would play a significant role in stepping up anti-rape activism on college campuses, and in inspiring the campus section of the Violence Against Women Act, which would be introduced into Congress five years later.

The survey questions were similar to those Koss used in the Kent State study. This time, however, she included a question about unwanted sexual intercourse that occurred because of the effects of alcohol or drugs. The results showed the extent to which sexual behavior in a college population had changed since Alfred Kinsey's male and female studies in the 1940s and 1950s. For example, the percentages of college-age males who were having sexual intercourse rose from 44 percent, reported by Kinsey, to 75 percent, reported by Koss in the 1980s. For college-age females, the percentages changed from 20 percent, reported by Kinsey, to 69 percent, reported by Koss. Morton Hunt, who conducted a survey of the sexual behavior of two thousand individuals in twenty-four cities in 1972, found a similar increase for college men, but a less marked increase for college women.

The results of Koss's national study were widely disseminated and quoted after publication in the *Journal of Consulting and Clinical Psychology* in 1987. Robin Warshaw's *I Never Called It Rape*, the first major book on acquaintance rape, was based on Koss's study. Warshaw reported that one in four women surveyed were victims of rape or attempted rape, 84 percent of those raped knew their attacker, and that 57 percent of the rapes happened on dates. The women thought that most of their offenders (73 percent) were drinking or using drugs at the time of the assault, and 55 percent admitted to using intoxicants themselves. Most of the women thought that they had made their nonconsent "quite" clear and that the offender used "quite a bit" of force. They resisted by using reasoning (84 percent) and physical struggle (70 percent). Only one quarter (27 percent) of the rape victims acknowledged themselves as such. Five percent reported their rapes to the police. Although many women did not call it rape, Koss reported that "the great majority of rape victims conceptualized their experience in highly negative terms and felt victimized whether or not they realized that legal standards for rape had been met."

The results for the men were similar to what Koss had found at Kent State. One quarter of the men reported involvement in some form of sexual aggression, ranging from unwanted touching to rape. Three percent admitted to attempted rape and 4.4 percent to rape. A high percentage of the males did not name their use of force as rape. Eighty-eight percent said it was definitely *not* rape. Forty-seven percent said they would do the same thing again.

Koss's findings that men viewed the use of force as normal were corroborated by other surveys conducted on college campuses. For example, one study cited by Russell found that 35 percent of the males questioned about the likelihood that they would rape said they might if they could get away with it. When asked whether they would force a female to do something sexual she really did not want to do, 60 percent of the males indicated in a third college study that they might, "given the right circumstances."

Convicted rapists hold similar beliefs. In a study of 114 rapists, Diana Scully found that many either denied that the sexual activity for which they were convicted was rape, or they claimed it hadn't happened. One told her the sexual activity for which he was convicted was "just fucking." Other rapists told her that men rape because they have learned that in America they can get away with it because victims don't report. Almost none of the convicts she interviewed thought they would go to prison. Most of them perceived rape as a rewarding, low-risk act.

Since the early studies conducted by Koss and Russell, a number of additional scientifically designed research studies conducted on campuses in various states and in various communities reveal that an average of between 13 percent and 25 percent of the participating females respond affirmatively to questions asking if they had ever been penetrated against their consent by a male who used force, threatened to use force, or took advantage of them when they were incapacitated with alcohol or other drugs. A more recent national study, published in 1992 by the National Victim Center, defined rape more narrowly by leaving alcohol and drugs out of the picture. Thirteen percent of this national sample of a cross-section of women reported having been victims of at least one completed rape in their lifetimes. Most of these women had been raped by someone they knew.

STRANGER RAPE

Patricia Rozee

Patricia Rozee is a psychology professor and the director of the Women's Studies Department at California State University in Long Beach. In the following selection, Rozee examines some of the similarities and differences between acquaintance rape and rape by a stranger. She writes that while stranger rapes and acquaintance rapes are equally traumatic, survivors of stranger rape are more likely than acquaintance rape victims to seek out help and report the assault. A woman who reports a rape by a stranger is more often believed than is a victim of acquaintance rape, Rozee maintains; however, women who engaged in allegedly provocative behavior may still be blamed for stranger rapes. Therapists and counselors should provide an accepting and supportive environment for rape survivors to help avoid casting blame on victims, Rozee recommends.

There is agreement among professionals, researchers, and activists that the majority of rapes, especially those that are unreported, are committed by dates or acquaintances. However, an estimated 20% to 50% of rapes each year are committed by strangers to the victim. Stranger rapes and acquaintance rapes are equally devastating to the victims. Stranger rape is generally thought to involve more force, display and use of weapons, and physical harm but also more resistance by the victim than acquaintance rape. There is a curvilinear relationship between the amount of violence used by the perpetrator and the degree of acquaintance between victim and perpetrator. Although there is a belief that the most violent rapes are stranger rapes, M. Koss, T. Dinero, C. Siebel & S. Cox found that the most violent are marital or familial rapes, followed by stranger rapes and then acquaintance rape.

S. Ullman and J. Siegel found no difference between stranger and acquaintance rape survivors in terms of ethnicity, age, income, education, or psychological symptoms. However, stranger rape survivors are more likely than acquaintance rape survivors to reach out to a friend, relative, or professional helper and are more likely to report the attack to the police.

Excerpted from Patricia Rozee, "Stranger Rape," in *The Psychology of Sexual Victimization: A Handbook*, edited by Michele Antoinette Paludi. Copyright © 1999 by Michele Antoinette Paludi. Reproduced with permission of Greenwood Publishing Group, Inc., Westport, CT.

Stranger rape differs in another way. It is stranger rape that women picture when they hear the word "rape." Stranger rapes are what S. Estrich refers to as "real rapes," meaning they are given more credibility and are more likely to receive legal remedies than are date or acquaintance rapes. Most people regard stranger rape as the more serious assault, including victims themselves, as evidenced by their greater reporting of stranger rape. Stranger rape victims are also more likely to label their experience as rape (53%) than are acquaintance rape victims (23%) or date rape victims. Women attribute more responsibility to victims of acquaintance rape than stranger rape, even when they are the victim. However, in virtually every study, men blame the victim more and identify with her less than do women, regardless of the type of rape.

Socially Condoned Rape

Rape is a socially constructed and socially legitimized phenomenon. Thus, even stranger rapes are often socially condoned or "normative." P. Rozee defines normative rape as genital contact that the female does not choose but is supported by social norms. In her random sample study of world societies, Rozee gives many examples of normative rape. Such socially approved rapes can be presumed when there is no punishment of the male; only the female is punished—for example, as "used goods"; rape is used as a punishment for errant females; rape is embedded in a cultural ritual such as an initiation ceremony or when the women's refusal would be punished by the community. Rozee concluded that rape is regulated, not prohibited, based on the finding that in most societies, there are examples of both normative and nonnormative (uncondoned) rapes operating concurrently. In nearly every society there are certain women whose rapes are not considered rape (e.g., wives, slaves, enemy women, prostitutes). As C. Muehlenhard and colleagues have pointed out, "As long as a society approves of or is silent about a form of sexual coercion, it is not considered rape."

Stranger rapes may be considered normative when jurors give undue weight to such extralegal factors as the victim's marital status, living arrangements, drinking patterns, and conformity to conservative gender role behaviors. In order to have suffered "real rape," a woman must be chaste, since prostitutes are considered unrapeable; have proof of penile penetration, since objects, fingers, and so on fall outside the legal definition of rape in most states; must show evidence of resisting, such as cuts and bruises, because without them, consent is implied; and should not have been involved in "provocative behavior," such as walking alone at night, wearing certain types of clothing, or consuming alcohol. Often the first question asked of a rape survivor is, "What were you doing out there by yourself?" or "What were you wearing?" or "Why did you let him in?" Each of these questions assumes that it was the victim's behavior that in some way caused or contributed to the assault. Rape law in the United States today, even when it involves rape by a stranger, is governed by the "law of exceptions." That is, rape is illegal, *except* when the victim dresses, looks, acts, or reacts in unacceptable ways. . . .

Rape and Power

According to L. Madigan and N. Gamble, rape is a reenactment of social dominance, no matter who the victim or the perpetrator is. Its motive is the subjugation of another person and demonstrates contempt and objectification of another. It is the acting out of power roles. Feminist theories that incorporate power analyses into explanations of rape can effectively explain both male-on-female rape and same-sex sexual assaults. Male power, domination, and physical force are part of the structure of U.S. society, but male-dominance theories are not sufficient to explain why most men do *not* rape or why there are female-perpetrated sexual assaults, as rare as these may be. That is because gender is but one of many power and status categories. Power roles can also be defined by economic status, physical size and strength, rank, or social status and be reinforced by personal traits such as aggressiveness, hostility, lack of empathy, and emotional unavailability.

Women's Fear of Rape

Women fear rape by male strangers, not by females or even by male dates. As R. Funk points out,

> Even though many men do not rape . . . and many are probably opposed to rape, all men benefit from rape and the constant threat of rape. If we benefit in no other way, we at least don't live with the constant threat of rape. . . . But all women are threatened, controlled, and victimized by the reality of rape and the constant threat that exists—represented by every man.

Thus, . . . women's fear of rape takes on special meaning because it is at its root a fear of stranger rape and has as a major consequence the social control of women.

Women's fear of rape results in their use of many self-imposed restrictive behaviors intended primarily to avoid rape. Women use more precautionary behaviors than men, and fear of rape is the best predictor of the use of isolation behaviors, such as not leaving the house. Women's fears are most likely to result in avoiding those activities they enjoy most, like visiting friends or going out for evening entertainment, because such behaviors are not "necessary." However, women also avoid night classes and night jobs if possible.

Women fear rape more than any other offense (including murder, assault, and robbery), and they report levels of fear three times higher than men's. Rozee reports a high fear of rape among both community and college women. On the single item, "I am scared of rape," 46 percent of women marked the highest possible agreement: 6 or 7 on a 7-point scale. On the item, "Rape would be devastating to my life," nearly half of the women marked the highest possible agreement levels.

P. Rozee, C. Wynne, D. Foster-Ogle, M. Compuesto, and M. Hsiao proposed a three-factor model to explain women's fear of rape. Their study demonstrates that the fear of the consequences of rape may be the essence of women's fear. Some of the most serious and immediate consequences that women fear are AIDS, injury, death, and mutilation. As well, they fear the psychological and emotional consequences: the fear of seeing the rapist again, nightmares, flashbacks and intrusive thoughts, feelings of powerlessness, negative effects on their sex life, hate and mistrust of men, and permanent life changes, including pregnancy.

The second most powerful predictor of women's fear of rape is the perception of exposure to risk. Higher fear was related to more exposure to sexual intrusions, such as sexual comments, obscene phone calls, being leered or whistled at, being followed or hassled on the street, being grabbed or fondled or rubbed up against, being exposed to flashers or masturbators, sexual harassment, rape situations, attempted and completed rapes, incest, and molestation. Higher fear was also related to receiving more warnings from parents, friends, and intimates about sexual danger. Although actual experience with fearful events is important, it seems that much of the perception about danger is related to respected other people's worries and communications about them.

The third predictor of women's fear of rape delineated by Rozee and colleagues was lack of perceived control. Women who lacked a strong internal locus of control over future events were more fearful of rape. There were no differences based on the ethnicity of the women on any of the major variables.

If the communication of danger by others is a major contributor to women's fear of rape, then it can be presumed that the way in which the media portray rape will have an effect on women's assessment of rape exposure. S. Brinson found 132 suggestions of rape myths in 26 rape episodes in a survey of prime-time dramas (five per episode). Most of the myths were of the type that reduces or denies the injury in rape and implies that the woman asked for it, wanted it, or lied about it. The news media are not much better, according to S. Riger and M. Gordon. A random sample survey of households conducted for the Census Bureau found that there are four attempted rapes for every one completed rape and that the press covers one attempted rape for every thirteen completed rapes that it covers. The press reports give the false impression that there are far more completed than attempted rapes, whereas the reverse is actually true. This is an important distinction because an attempted rape is a situation where a woman fought back and was not raped. If the Census Bureau figures are correct, then women are four times more likely to escape their would-be rapists than they are to be raped. The media reporting gives women the impression that they are 13 times more likely to be raped than to escape a would-be rapist. An attempted rape is not "news." Such sensationalist reporting does a disservice to women by exaggerating women's helplessness, instilling a lack of self-confidence in their ability to defend themselves, and thus increasing fear of rape.

The finding that other people's warnings exacerbate fear of rape coupled with the impression of the pervasiveness of rape given by the media demonstrate that firsthand experience with rape is not needed to instill a fear of rape among women. Even in societies where rape is rare, the concept of rape as communicated through folk tales (where a fictional person is punished by being raped) is enough to keep women in their place and fearful. . . .

Coping with Rape

Survivors of stranger rape and acquaintance rapes are equally devastated. While some older studies showed that some women, particularly Asian-American women and Latinas, had more difficult recoveries, recent comparisons find no ethnic differences in the impact of rape. Some studies have found that stranger rape seems to be related to greater depression and fear, while others have found no difference in mental health outcomes among date, stranger, and marital rape survivors.

It is important to remember that not all victims are equally traumatized by a rape. There is considerable variability in response, and a number of factors (e.g. social support, community resources) may mediate the impact of rape. Many rape survivors can be expected to suffer problems in sexual function, intimate relationships, fear, and depression for sometimes years later. There may also be problems in self-esteem and self-efficacy and lowered affect.

Some women resist the label of rape because the personal or cultural meaning they attach to it is intolerable. These researchers also point out that it is not necessary for a survivor to acknowledge rape to begin the process of recovery.

Interventions with Rape Survivors

According to M. Koss and B. Burkhart, few victims are willing to accept immediate postrape therapeutic intervention, preferring to put it out of mind and go on. They found that 31% to 48% of victims eventually sought professional psychotherapy, often years after the assault. G. Wyatt reports that of those incidents of sexual assault that were not disclosed to anyone until years later, 64% involved African-American women as compared to 36% for white women. Such delays can have negative effects on recovery and result in elevated levels of use of mental health services later on. Failure to disclose reduces access to resources and results in a lack of social support for the victim. Koss and Burkhart suggest that the primary role of clinicians may be in the identification and handling of chronic, posttraumatic responses to an event that is long past. However, they also point out that most of the literature addresses immediate postrape symptoms.

Some of the general goals that therapists and others can work toward with survivors of sexual assault have been outlined by I. Schwartz:

1. Provide accurate information regarding sexual assault, focusing on societal blame rather than self-blame.
2. Promote healthy relationships and support systems.
3. Encourage positive actions she can take on her own behalf.
4. Help her set goals for herself and follow through on them.
5. Emphasize that you understand the challenges posed by rape and that recovery means increased strength, personal growth, and self-reliance for the majority of women.

Madigan and Gamble remind us that therapists can revictimize rape victims if they are ignorant and unwilling to accept the woman's reality once she tells it. It is difficult to hear a woman's rape story. Helpers must fight the tendency to distance themselves from victims by using feelings of personal invulnerability ("it can never happen to me because . . ."), searching for psychosexual motives, or viewing the rape as an individual problem, to the exclusion of viewing it as primarily a societal problem. Therapists must address their own feelings of disbelief. The attitudes of rape crisis counselors, emergency room workers, police officers, and other helpers will often influence a victim's opinions about whether it was "real rape." They must avoid trying to make the rape rational, to explain the unexplainable. One of the main components in most stranger rapes is sheer chance—being in the wrong place at the wrong time. It is important for those working with rape survivors to examine their own belief systems about rape, especially victim-blaming rape myths. Many men and some women believe rape myths to some degree. Maintaining a supportive nonstigma view of rape as a crime helps avoid victim blaming. . . .

Since rape survivors are reluctant to contact mental health professionals immediately after rape, it is important to provide information for lay helpers, who may be the persons of first resort. P. Tyra suggests the following guidelines for nontherapist helpers of rape survivors:

1. Be concerned and available.
2. Give the woman time to ventilate about the experience.
3. Help put the rape into perspective. She is not to blame.
4. Give information about resources and referrals.
5. Help identify emotionally supportive people in her life.
6. Offer to telephone the next day to see how she is feeling.

Sometimes there is no better help than simply a good listener with a calm and caring manner. . . .

Factors Affecting Recovery

M. Koss and T. Mukai point to a number of factors that have not been adequately studied for their effects on the recovery process, including the effect of participating in the criminal justice system, the effectiveness of the type of counseling provided, social support, coping methods by the victim, and victim attributions.

One area that has received considerable study is the effect of active resistance by the intended victim on her physical and psychological outcomes. In 1985, P. Bart and P. O'Brien published the first large-scale study on successful survival strategies for women facing rape. Their work was significant in that it challenged, with data, the common notion that a woman should not fight a rapist because she would be hurt worse. Many police officers also share the common assumption that those who fight back get hurt more, but recent studies dispute this view.

Current research on self-defense concludes *unequivocally* that:

1. Women who fight back and fight back immediately are less likely to be raped than women who do not.
2. Women who fight back are no more likely to be injured than women who do not fight back. In fact, it has been shown that victim resistance often occurred *in response to* physical attack.
3. Pleading, begging, and reasoning are ineffective in preventing rape or physical injury.
4. Women who fight back experience less postassault symptomology due to avoidance of being raped.
5. Women who fought back had faster psychological recoveries whether or not they were raped.
6. Fighting back strengthens the physical evidence should the survivor decide to prosecute for rape or attempted rape.

S. Ullman and R. Knight also dispute the idea that physical resistance provokes increased violence in particular types of rapists, such as sadists. Based on a sample of incarcerated stranger rapists, their study showed that overall, the efficacy of women's resistance strategies for avoiding sexual abuse and physical injury did not vary by rapist type. Women who fought in response to sadistic rapists were no more likely to experience physical injury than women who did not. Ullman and Knight admonish people from issuing warnings against the supposed dangers of physical resistance to sadistic rapists in the absence of any empirical data to support such claims. They also point out the futility of advising women to assess the "type" of rapist before determining whether to resist.

Victim resistance raises the cost of rape for the perpetrator. It makes rape completion more difficult, increases the effort required by the rapist, and prolongs the attack, thereby increasing the risk of discovery and capture. It also increases the probability of injury to the rapist, possibly leaving marks that will contribute to late discovery.

Given the prevalence of rape, it would seem that warning women not to fight back because they might get hurt is based in myth, not empirical evidence. Cooperation with the assailant does not guarantee safety and resistance does not increase risk. Such myths serve only to ensure more victims for would-be rapists, and they do an immense disservice to women by absurdly encouraging them to "bargain" with criminals. Only 3% of rapes involve some additional injury that is serious; usually the rape itself is the most serious injury suffered. Thus, the myth that fighting back will get you hurt mistakes from where the real hurt comes: trying to recover from rape.

RAPE AS A TACTIC OF WAR

Barbara Crossette

Throughout several ethnic conflicts in the 1990s, rape was committed as a deliberate tactic of war, reports Barbara Crossette in the following selection. In the Balkans, Rwanda, and Indonesia, she writes, soldiers used premeditated sexual assault as a means to terrorize and disgrace their enemy's civilian population. Rape has not been an unusual occurrence during wars, Crossette states, but the motivation has changed: During the recent wars, rape became a veritable tool of ethnic conflict, she maintains. In response to the atrocities, international tribunals and other groups concerned with human rights have decided to define these rapes as war crimes. Crossette is a staff writer for the *New York Times*.

They strike without warning, bringing terror to an apartment in Algeria, a Chinese shop in Indonesia, a squalid refugee encampment in Africa or a Balkan farming village under siege. They are shadowy men with causes so blinding and hatreds so deep that they have transformed modern warfare into orgies of primordial savagery—raping, brutalizing, humiliating, slashing and hacking women and girls to death.

More civilians than soldiers are being maimed and killed in the wars of nationalism and ethnicity that are the hallmark of the 20th century's end, wars fought in neighborhoods rather than battlefields.

More to the point, it is becoming increasingly apparent that the new style of warfare is often aimed specifically at women and is defined by a view of premeditated, organized sexual assault as a tactic in terrorizing and humiliating a civilian population. In some cases the violators express a motive that seems to have more in common with the tactics of ancient marauding hordes than with the 20th century—achieving forced pregnancy and thus poisoning the womb of the enemy.

From Bosnia to Indonesia

International attention first focused on the use of rape as a tactic of warfare in Bosnia, where a United Nations commission and human rights groups found that ethnic Serb paramilitary groups had systematically tolerated or encouraged the raping of Bosnian Muslim women

Reprinted from Barbara Crossette, "An Old Scourge of War Becomes Its Latest Crime," *The New York Times*, June 14, 1998. Reprinted with permission from *The New York Times*.

as part of the effort to drive Muslims from their homes and villages between 1991 and 1995.

Rape was also employed by Hutu troops against Tutsi women in the genocidal campaign Hutu leaders conducted in Rwanda in 1994. In 1997, women who identified with secular culture in Algeria accused desperate rebels fighting in the name of Islamic revolution of kidnapping them and making them sex slaves. In Indonesia, reports are surfacing that suggest members of the security forces may have been among the men who raped ethnic Chinese women during rioting in May 1998.

And in 1998 in the Balkans, Serbs were again emptying towns of a rival ethnic group—this time Albanians in Kosovo—and human rights and women's groups were monitoring the growing violence for the possibility that rape would again be one of the techniques.

None of this is the essentially random rape that traditionally follows conquest, intolerable though that is; it is different even from forcing conquered women to be prostitutes for the victors, as Japan did in Korea during World War II.

The difference is that in all four recent cases, sexual degradation and intimidation—often public—seem to have been used as a strategy of ethnic or religious conflict itself.

This use of rape as a premeditated act of warfare is challenging anew the efforts by nations of the world to organize effectively to prevent and punish crimes against humanity, a monumental task that moves into new territory with the 1998 opening of a treaty conference in Rome to create the world's first international criminal court. Largely because of the systematic use of sexual assault in ethnic wars in the Balkans and Rwanda, the court is expected to rank rape as an internationally recognized war crime for the first time in history, alongside violence against noncombatants, mistreatment of prisoners, torture and other unusual punishments.

The Rape Camps

Widney Brown, an advocate with the women's rights division of Human Rights Watch, echoed other experts when she said that rape "has probably been an issue in every major conflict, but what happened in Bosnia, particularly with the creation of the rape camps, really brought it to light." In the Balkans, where soldiers of every faction were accused of rape, the discovery of areas where Serbian soldiers confined Bosnian Muslim women to be raped shocked many. "In Yugoslavia rape was a part of ethnic cleansing, because the message that you got was if you stayed, the men would be murdered and the women would be raped," Ms. Brown said.

"That was followed very quickly by what happened in Rwanda, where we have similar widespread allegations of rape and mutilation," she added.

In fact, part of the preliminary campaign that created the atmosphere that allowed the genocide to happen was the demonization of Tutsi women as oversexualized creatures who were seductresses. It's not surprising that during the conflict they were subjected to rape, and a lot of sexual mutilation. Mutilation is another way of saying, "We don't perceive of this person as a human being."

For more than five years now, ad hoc tribunals have been hearing allegations of war crimes, first in the Balkans and later in Rwanda, and these tribunals have already decided to consider rape a war crime in those conflicts. Since they have been serving as small-scale models for the permanent international court that is just being formed, that court is expected to follow suit.

"These tribunals were literally forced to pay attention to a series of petitions and pressures from women's organizations demanding that rape be recognized," said Felice Gaer, an expert on human rights and international organizations for the American Jewish Committee. Ms. Gaer said that ultimately the support of Justice Richard Goldstone, the first war crimes prosecutor for the Balkans and Rwanda, succeeded in elevating sex crimes to the level of genocide and crimes against humanity. This was the first step taken by nations trying to tackle collectively this new scourge of war. But women are drawing up a longer list of gender-related crimes in wartime, and promise a battle to have them recognized by the International Criminal Court.

Ken Franzblau, who tracks the sexual exploitation of women for Equality Now, a New York-based organization that aids women in poor nations and immigrant women here, said rape is so widespread now because it is so effective in ethnic wars.

"It has such devastating effects on communities, particularly in traditional societies or very religious communities where the virginity and the fidelity of women can be central to the makeup of that society," he said. Rape is a psychological grenade thrown into the middle of daily life to provoke maximum terror. "That's why you see a fair number of these rapes committed in front of family members of the girls or women involved," he said.

Some analysts believe that the fast pace of international communications today may be a factor in the rapid recurrence of the use of rape as a tactic of war in such widely separate parts of the world. But if that is true, it is also evident that rapid international communication has played a role in stirring international outrage about the tactic.

Over the last decade, there have been significant changes among the vulnerable women themselves. Women who were the victims of sexual abuse in the name of ethnic purity, nationalism and sometimes religious zeal have begun to speak out, often aided by human rights organizations and women's crisis centers. For many, this has been a revolutionary change.

Beyond Suicide

"Lots of women just committed suicide in the past," said Charlotte Bunch, executive director of the Center for Women's Global Leadership at Rutgers.

> That's one very clear thing that's beginning to emerge now. In this decade, the outrage that women have been able to raise about the issue means that people are reporting it. But the truth is that there is also a backlash about women speaking out. There may be some moments before we reach a point where there is enough outrage to get the phenomenon under control.

The phenomenon takes human form in a number of recent accounts reported by journalists. Take the story of Nawal Fathi, who was captured by militants in Algeria in 1996, made into a sex slave and raped by a score of men before being rescued by government troops. A psychiatrist who treated her said that despite a year of medical treatment, Ms. Fathi committed suicide at the age of 24 in 1997.

In Jakarta in 1998, aid workers were quoted as saying that hundreds of ethnic Chinese women had been sexually assaulted during the looting of Chinese neighborhoods, apparently by organized gangs that may have had links to security forces. "Some of the attackers said, 'You must be raped because you are Chinese and non-Muslim,'" one woman recalled. Again, a number of women have killed themselves rather than live in shame.

Outside Religion

Although militants in Algeria and roving gangs of rapists in Indonesia are Muslims, the phenomenon is probably not related to religion, though radical religious views may provide justification to an elemental misogyny. The Taliban movement in Afghanistan, for example, has repressed women but its holy warriors have not abused them sexually, as their predecessors in the Mujahedeen armies were frequently accused of doing, Afghan women say. Roman Catholics butchered other Roman Catholics in Rwanda and Burundi. Sex slaves are also a hallmark of the vaguely evangelical Lord's Resistance Army in Uganda. Burmese troops in Myanmar, a Buddhist country, are accused in a report from the human-rights group Earthrights of using rape as a weapon against women from 20 or more ethnic minorities or student groups that oppose the military regime.

Because women displaced by ethnic warfare or other forms of mass violence are often not safe even in refugee camps—or arrive there pregnant through rape—United Nations relief agencies and some private groups have begun to offer gynecological services and the "morning after" pill, which prevents conception. Although this practice has been sharply criticized by anti-abortion groups in the United States, the United Nations High Commissioner for Refugees, Sadako

Ogata, and others have continued to provide help to abused women.

At Equality Now, Mr. Franzblau said the kind of sexual abuse that took place in Bosnia, where Serb rapes of Muslim women were numerous and intense personal hatred was directed at neighbors, not some distant stranger at an enemy gun emplacement, makes the impact much worse and stokes the fires for the next round of strife.

"That's why it is going to be very difficult to reconcile these communities," he said. "How can you move families back to homes where a mother or daughter or sister was raped by a next-door neighbor?"

UNCOVERING MALE-ON-MALE RAPE

Michael Scarce

The majority of rape victims are women, but men do comprise between 5 and 10 percent of all reported rapes in any given year, writes Michael Scarce in the following selection. Most male rape victims are assaulted in or near their homes by a heterosexual man they know, Scarce points out, and weapons are used more often in male rape than in the rape of women. He explains that men who are raped face the same kind of shame and emotional upheaval experienced by female victims, but men are more likely to deny that their rape occurred. The societal myth that men are not raped causes most male rape victims to decide not to report the attack, Scarce writes; moreover, some men fear that admitting they were raped will raise questions about their sexual orientation. The lack of resources for male victims contributes to the myth that men are not raped and often makes it more difficult for them to recover, the author maintains. Scarce is the author of *Male on Male Rape: The Hidden Toll of Stigma and Shame.*

Several months after I was raped, I felt a strong need to learn more about rape and sexual violence in an attempt to make sense of what had happened to me. In part, this feeling was related to a sense of isolation. At that time I knew of no other men who had been sexually assaulted, but I believed I must not be the only person to have endured the experience of same-sex sexual violence. When I returned to campus my junior year at Ohio State, I headed directly to the library and spent many hours searching for any and all literature related to adult male rape. I found plenty of articles and books written on the subject of childhood assault, but very little on the rape of adult males. What little I did uncover was highly academic and impersonal, articles from scholarly journals that did not resonate with me on an emotional or practical level. Over time I have collected and photocopied every newspaper, magazine, and research article that I have come across in hopes of piecing together a larger picture of men raping men. . . .

A Bit of History

Within the broader context of physical assault, men are more likely than women to be victims of violent crimes. Rape and domestic violence are two of the few exceptions to this likelihood, and the popular perception that rape is a form of violence committed only against women has contributed to the lack of writings published on the topic of male rape. Academic research on male rape has been conducted only since the late 1970s with any regularity, first bolstered by feminist social movements that directed attention toward sexual violence. Although the majority of this attention involved men raping women, the development and dissemination of the idea that rape is an exercise in power began to shed light on the rape of men as well, particularly in prisons and other correctional facilities.

In her landmark book published in 1975, *Against Our Will*, feminist scholar Susan Brownmiller included an essay on the same-sex rape of men in prisons, making connections between the differences in power that exist between men and women as parallel to the power imbalance between men in single-sex institutions: "Prison rape is generally seen today for what it is: an acting out of power roles within an all-male, authoritarian environment in which the weaker, younger inmate, usually a first offender, is forced to play the role that in the outside world is assigned to women." Growing attention to the rape of men in prisons created a public acknowledgment that men can, and are, sexually assaulted by other men, opening the door for other men to step forward and report they had been raped outside of prison walls. The resulting recognition that rape in prison may differ in significant ways from rape outside of prison soon attracted the interest of a handful of social scientists.

In his 1979 book *Men Who Rape*, psychologist Nicholas Groth devoted 22 pages of his work to men who raped, or had been raped by, other men, reflecting the growing recognition of male rape among researchers and academics. This section of Groth's book marks a noteworthy departure from the previous research that had been conducted on same-sex rape in that the majority of rape survivors he interviewed were assaulted in such nonprison settings as hitchhiking along highways, outdoors in the woods or at a beach, on the street, in the victim's home, in a parking garage, and at the victim's place of employment. Whereas past work had focused almost entirely on rape and its relationship to homosexuality behind bars, Groth's interviews laid important groundwork for a contemporary understanding of the larger picture of power dynamics and sexual violence between men in noninstitutional community settings through his case study analyses.

Apart from some of the theoretical essays such as Susan Brownmiller's that delve into the social meanings attached to male rape, the majority of published work on men raping men is more quantitative in nature—counting and measuring aspects of the rape of men. The investigators who have studied male rape have been primarily grounded in the fields of psychology, criminology, and epidemiology, and for the most part have been located in the United States and England. Taken as a whole, the approximately 20 studies that have been published in the last three decades often yield conflicting results and draw contradictory conclusions in their quantification of the details of male rape. . . .

The Larger Picture

An overview of this body of research reveals certain trends and recurrent themes, and simultaneously draws attention to the weaknesses and omissions of the knowledge that has been generated from such inquiry. Although a great deal of progress has been made in investigating male rape, there are still many voids and unanswered questions. What few generalizations have been formulated about the rape of men offer a glimpse of the breadth and depth this violence bears. The following summaries of male rape characteristics are an extrapolation of this body of research, generating a larger picture of the problem.

Incidence and prevalence. Incidence can be defined as the number of new rapes that have occurred in a given time period among a certain population, whereas prevalence refers to the number of rapes that have ever occurred among a population. In terms of incidence, studies of male rape in the United States and United Kingdom indicate that somewhere between 5 and 10% of all reported rapes in any given year involve male victims. The number and percentage of rapes involving male victims is presumably much higher than this, however, as this estimate reflects only *reported* rapes. Several researchers, including Arthur Kaufman of the University of New Mexico School of Medicine and Deryck Calderwood, the former director of the Human Sexuality Program at New York University, have indicated that male rape survivors are much less likely to report their rape victimization than are female survivors.

Some of the evidence supporting this estimation of 5 to 10% includes:

- In 1982, Dr. Bruce Forman of the University of South Dakota School of Medicine published his research findings on 212 rape victims in South Carolina, 5.7% of whom were male.
- In a large-scale study called the Los Angeles Epidemiologic Catchment Area Project conducted in 1987, 7% of the males reported having been sexually assaulted at least once as an adult.
- Of the 528 clients seen at the San Francisco Rape Treatment Center in 1990, 9.8% were men.
- In 1992, the Sexual Assault Center in Hartford, Connecticut, logged 400 calls from men out of a total of 4058.
- In 1993, Margaret Henderson, director of the Orange County Rape Crisis Center in North Carolina, reported that 7% of the 147 victims assisted at her agency were men.

- The Ohio Coalition on Sexual Assault, polling rape crisis organizations across their state in 1994, found males to constitute 7% of clients served.
- Of the average 250 rape survivors seen each year at Beth Israel Hospital's rape crisis program, about 10% are male.
- According to the Bureau of Justice Statistics' National Crime Victimization Survey, of the rapes reported to the survey in 1994, 5% of rape victims aged 12 and older were males (1994 is the most recent year for which these data are available).
- In addition to the above findings, this 5 to 10% range has been confirmed by other studies.

Rapists. The sexual orientation of men who rape other men tends to be heterosexual (either self-identified or as later identified by the men they assault). The rapists are usually in their early to mid-20s at the time of the assault, and are primarily white. Virtually every study indicates that men rape other men out of anger or an attempt to overpower, humiliate, and degrade their victims rather than out of lust, passion, or sexual desire.

Victims. Men who are raped by other men tend to be in their late teens to late 20s at the time of assault. In terms of race, when noted in research studies, African-American male rape survivors in these studies were overrepresented relative to the percentage of African Americans in the communities in which the studies were conducted. In terms of sexual orientation, when documented in research studies, gay men seem to have been raped at much higher rates than heterosexual men.

Assaults. As for the rapist and victim relationship, research studies draw conflicting conclusions regarding the predominance of stranger or acquaintance rape. At a 1996 conference on male rape at DeMontfort University in England, Michael King, head of psychiatry at the Royal Free School of Medicine, presented his research findings that male rape victims are usually attacked in their homes by someone they know. This correlates with earlier studies indicating that weapons are frequently used in male rape, and at a much higher frequency than in the rape of women. Perhaps rapists feel they need an additional form of power to rape other men, whereas psychological fear and intimidation may be enough to overpower many women. Even if a weapon is not used, some use of force or threat of force is almost invariably employed, except in cases where the victim is asleep or unconscious. Multiple assailants also seem to be more prevalent in the rape of men than women. With regard to anatomical site in male rape cases, virtually every study of male rape survivors found that anal penetration of the victim was the most common form of assault. Oral penetration was the next most common assault of men. In some instances, the assailant took the victim's penis into his own mouth or anus, or masturbated the victim. Several studies and news media stories include reports of an attacker forcing one male victim to penetrate another male victim.

The Impact on the Victim

There is no single, typical, emotional response that every man will exhibit after he has been assaulted. Some may appear calm and rational, others may exhibit anger, depression, or hysteria. Still others may socially withdraw and appear nonresponsive. All of these behaviors should be deemed normal, as each individual will react to crisis situations in ways that are related to his own identity, culture, and background. Several of the following reactions overlap and intersect, such as anger and self-blame, for example.

Stigma and shame. Perhaps the most powerful effect of male rape is the stigma, shame, and embarrassment that follows as survivors begin to cope with what has happened to them. The role of self-blame in this shame is prominent, as many male survivors feel a sense of guilt for their assault and feel embarrassed that they were in some way responsible for their victimization. The involvement of body parts that our culture deems to be "sexual" or "private" may also hamper survivors' ability to speak openly about their experience. The general public's equation of rape with sex may also bring on a shame attached to homosexuality. Nathan, a rape survivor I interviewed, explained, "I'm not sure I'll ever tell any of my family or my friends. They would probably understand, but I'd just be too embarrassed. I'd always be wondering if they thought less of me."

Guilt. Shame is most often accompanied by a sense of guilt. Many rape survivors feel as if some action on their part provoked the rape, or that they did not effectively resist to avoid the rape altogether. Usually the shame and stigma mentioned above stems from some form of this guilt and self-blame. As one survivor I interviewed expressed, "It really upset me that I let him do that to me. I can't believe I didn't find a way to make it stop at some point while it was happening. I should've been able to, I really should have." Male survivors' sense of self-blame is not entirely internal, unfortunately. All too often, the friends, family, and service providers of male rape survivors project their judgment of responsibility on the survivor. Marcus, a man who was raped is his early 20s, told me that his rape "began a period, which continues to the present day, almost 5 years now, of a declining relationship with my mother. She bitterly fought against me and the idea that it had happened. When she did kind of admit it had happened, it suddenly became my fault."

Rape trauma syndrome and posttraumatic stress disorder. Rape trauma syndrome, a form of posttraumatic stress disorder, was first described in 1974 as a condition affecting female survivors of sexual assault. Professor of Nursing Ann Burgess and Professor of Sociology Dr. Larry Holmstrom at Boston College, who specialize in the research and treatment of sexual violence, initially coined the term *rape trauma syndrome*. They divided the syndrome into two distinct phases: acute and long term. The acute phase is marked by a period of extreme disorganization and upheaval in the survivor's life following the rape. Some of the impact reactions during the acute phase are: physical trauma, skeletal muscle tension, gastrointestinal irritability, genitourinary disturbance, and a wide gamut of emotional reactions. The long-term phase consists of survivors' attempt to reorganize their lifestyles. The impacted reactions most noted in this phase are: increased motor activity (such as changing residence or traveling for support), disturbing dreams and nightmares, and "traumatophobia," which includes such responses as fear of indoors if the survivor was raped in bed, fear of outdoors if the survivor was raped outside of his home, fear of being alone, fear of crowds, fear of people walking behind him, and a fear of engaging in or resuming consensual sexual activity. Since the initial identification of rape trauma syndrome in 1974, psychological and legal researchers have extended the condition to male survivors as well. In a 1989 study by Michael Myers, a psychiatrist with the Department of Psychiatry at the University of British Columbia, Vancouver, the most common form of psychiatric diagnoses was posttraumatic stress disorder. Dr. Myers described in detail one of his patients, whom he calls "Mr. B":

> Mr. B had flashbacks of the repeated acts of sodomy, rectal pain, nightmares of suffocation and death, and marked detachment from his family and friends. He suffered weeks of initial insomnia and fears of sleeping alone. Showering became an ordeal for him as he feared someone behind the shower curtain attacking him. In order to sleep, he had to lay on his side—lying prone or supine made him feel vulnerable to another attack.

Andrew, a survivor I interviewed who was raped by multiple assailants, explained similar effects that continue to haunt him:

> I don't think I ever leave my house without feeling some fear. Even if I don't consciously think about it, there's that sense within me that I'm at risk, especially when it's dark. I'm very hypervigilant. Nothing goes on around me that I'm not aware of. I have a hard time even paying attention. I get distracted very easily because I'm always watching. At night when I go out I am very careful about where I go. Everywhere I go I have plotted out in my mind very quickly an escape route. That if I feel threatened, I know I've already calculated it's only this many steps to here where I know it would be safe, or there are people over here and if I holler loud enough they'll hear me. I had a security system put in my house and the minute I come

home I turn it on. I still wake up in the middle of the night, terrified. I wake up with that taste in my mouth. I can taste it again, that smell again. Sometimes at night I wake up and— the pain, anally—it feels like a knife going through me to where I almost jump straight up. When that happens, the nights are still pretty hard. I usually don't go back to sleep.

A study of 22 male rape survivors conducted by researcher P. L. Huckle at the South Wales Forensic Psychiatric Service found similar patterns of posttraumatic stress disorder. The effects of rape trauma syndrome can last a lifetime, especially in the absence of therapeutic treatment and a strong social support system from family or loved ones. . . .

Hostility and anger. In one comparative study of male and female rape survivors at the Hennepin County Medical Center in Minneapolis, psychologist Patricia Frazier discovered that male survivors were rated as more depressed and hostile than female survivors immediately following the rape. Other studies have reported similar findings. A man who has been raped may feel a great deal of anger toward the rapist, toward those support persons closest to him after the assault, toward a society that does not recognize or validate his experience, toward service providers who are inadequately prepared to meet his needs, or toward himself for not preventing the assault in the first place. Although anger can certainly be a healthy and valid reaction to sexual violence, survivors may need assistance in managing their anger by channeling it into productive action.

A Desire to Control One's Reactions

Denial. One study conducted at a hospital emergency room in New Mexico found male survivors were more likely than female survivors to use denial and control their reactions to the assault. . . . Denial may serve a male survivor who is incapable of managing the reality of his assault. Denial of male rape may be much easier for men than women, as the rape of men is rarely addressed in highly public ways. If there is a general belief in our society that male rape is either impossible or never happens, there is little challenge or contradiction to a male survivor's attempt to refute his rape experience. Denial becomes an especially easy and effective tool for avoiding the emotional pain and traumatic memory of sexual violation. Marcus, a rape survivor I interviewed, remembered:

I pretty rapidly had moved into a state of denial about its effects on my life even though I look back on that period now and see how tense I was all the time, how I started to pull in and really resist involvement in many important parts of my whole life. I kept walking around afraid that everybody could sort of see what had happened. I stayed in that condition for about 9 months and really just feeling, like, I'm fine. So I didn't even talk with too many people about it.

Even a lack of resources or professionals who specialize in the treatment and recovery of male rape survivors may reinforce a conclusion that because male rape remains hidden, it must not really exist. Survivors may be able to easily self-identify with the invisibility of male rape to the point of not recognizing or acknowledging their experience altogether. Later in my interview with Marcus, he told me that calling the local rape crisis hotline had never entered his mind as an available option:

> A friend of mine was a rape counselor. It never even occurred
> to her that I should call a crisis line and it never occurred to
> me until years later. I think it's because it was Bay Area
> *Women* Against Rape. That's probably the main reason—the
> focus of the crisis line is towards women and a lot of the
> counselors don't believe the agency serves men even though
> they are told explicitly that [the agency] does. And it never
> occurred to me to call, because it's a women's organization.
> On an intellectual level I knew that this happened to other
> people. On an emotional level I felt like it didn't happen to
> any other men and that somehow I was unique because of
> that and therefore there wouldn't be anything set up for me.

Depression. Varying levels of depression from mild to severe are highly common among survivors of sexual violence. Understandably, the impact of sexual violence may leave many men unable to cope with a perceived loss of manhood, sexual dysfunction, shame, or isolation. In association with some forms of depression, many rape survivors "self-medicate" by consuming alcohol or other drugs to relieve their anguish. As one survivor of prison wrote in a letter to the anti-rape organization Stop Prisoner Rape, "Today, like every day since I 'died' in a pool of my own blood, I am nothing more than a mannequin of flesh and bone, void of normal feelings, and hopelessly obsessed with cocaine in an effort to medicate my simple mind to oblivion." Issues of addiction, increased risk of HIV infection, consideration of suicide, or unintentional injury may become some of the many key areas of concern in treatment of rape-related depression. . . .

T.J., a male rape survivor I interviewed, told me of an experience during his college years in which he stumbled upon a friend, also a male rape survivor, who was seriously contemplating suicide:

> We were living in this dorm. Next door to us was this really
> good friend of mine who I had met at the campus Gay and
> Lesbian Alliance meetings, Bob. So one day my roommate
> and I knocked on Bob's door and then walked into his room.
> He was sitting there holding a gun. We said, "What's going
> on?" He said, "I'm trying to decide whether to shoot myself

or not." We said, "What?" He said, "Yeah, I'm sick of getting raped all the time. In every relationship I've been in, at some point or another, I've been raped. It started when my dad raped me." He was in agony. He and I became good friends, and we started processing things together.

When I interviewed Andrew, he told me of the night he was raped and his resulting intent to just give up on life:

> I got back home and I was lost. I felt pretty sure I was going to kill myself. I was pretty convinced I would do that before the night was over. There was something about the fact that I didn't want to see morning. I had enough pills at home that I knew I could do it from my training, what to take.

Even though Andrew made it through that first night after he was raped, he continues to consider suicide and told me:

> At times when I'm laying in bed, I wake up and I feel like there's someone standing there. I'm so scared I can't even roll over to look. I can't move. I try to tell myself, your alarm system's on, if anyone came in, you would know it. And none of that matters. I can't move. During those times at night I still think about suicide. I have over 700 pills here in a lock box, probably enough to commit suicide 10 to 12 times over. Some nights when that happens I wake up and I think "You don't have to go through this anymore."

Unfortunately, the contemplation and act of suicide is fairly common among male rape survivors, especially those who do not feel they can reach out for the support they so desperately need.

The Shock of Being Raped

Surprise. The outright surprise and shock of being raped may be dramatically higher for men than women. From the time when women are very young girls, our society teaches them to anticipate the possibility of rape and normalize the sexual violence of women as an unfortunate fact of life. Women routinely live their lives on the defense by altering their behavior to avoid assault—doing everything from not walking alone at night to changing the way they dress so as not to "invite" violent behavior from men. Few men are trained to be aware of their vulnerability to sexual assault, however, which may seem beyond the realm of most men's reality. After all, male rape is largely ignored by the media, public health outreach, and other educational endeavors. When a man realizes he has been sexually assaulted, it is understandable for him to feel as if he is the only one to ever undergo such an experience given this widespread invisibility. This is illustrated by the earlier quote from Marcus, who said that he felt like no other men were raped and that he was unique in his victimization. The following quotes from survivors, reported in various psychological studies, illustrate this disbelief:

> I don't think a lot of people believe it could happen . . . I'm 6'2" and weigh 220 pounds.

> I didn't know what they [the assailants] had in mind. Rape was the furthest thing from my mind. The furthest.

> As his hand went to my belt, I was motionless with disbelief. "What's going on?" I thought.

Conflicting sense of sexual orientation. Some men who have been raped may interpret their experience as an act of sex, concluding they have had a homosexual encounter. This may lead some men to question their sexual identity in an attempt to make sense of their assault experience. If a male rape survivor is treated with homophobia by those he confides in, he may adopt the label of "gay" that others inappropriately impose on him. Some gay male rape survivors may feel they were targeted for sexual violence because of sexual orientation, and may attempt to deny or hide their sexual identity so as to safeguard themselves from future assault.

Body image and self-esteem. In relation to depression and self-blame, survivors may feel as if their bodies are permanently damaged in the eyes of others, less than their former selves as a result of their assault. Often these feelings manifest themselves in the form of low self-esteem and a lack of self-worth, as well as negative changes in perception of body image.

Heightened sense of vulnerability. As with any victimization of violent crime, male rape survivors may experience a heightened sense of vulnerability in their everyday lives, hyperconscious and overly aware of the possibility of future attacks. This may occur as a component of the rape trauma syndrome discussed earlier.

Although the above list of survivor reactions to rape is not exhaustive, it gives a strong indication of just how dramatically sexual violence can alter a man's life. As more research is conducted on male rape, especially in the disciplines of psychology and psychiatry, these responses will be more closely studied and, hopefully, better forms of gender-specific treatment will become available to accommodate the immediate and lasting effects of rape.

DANGEROUS DATE-RAPE DRUGS

Joan Zorza

In the following selection, Joan Zorza discusses the dangerous effects of Rohypnol and Gamma-hydroxybutyrate (GHB), two fast-acting depressants that are gaining increasing notoriety as "date-rape drugs." In large enough dosages, each of these drugs can cause extreme muscle weakness, unconsciousness, and amnesia, Zorza reports. Rapists can slip these drugs into a drink to incapacitate their victims, who will often have no memory of the attack. Furthermore, the author writes, these drugs exit the body quickly and leave no long-term evidence of ingestion, thereby making it more difficult for victims to prove that they were drugged and raped. Zorza advises women to protect themselves by avoiding beverages that taste or look unusual or that have been left unattended. Zorza is the editor of *Sexual Assault Report*, a bimonthly newsletter written for professionals who assist and treat victims of sexual violence.

Reading the social science literature on sexual assault and rape, one might never know that the drugs Rohypnol and Gamma-hydroxybutyrate [GHB] exist, or that other date-rape drugs exist. Similarly, one would probably not know, except for seeing an occasional newspaper story or reports following legislation, that these drugs are a rapist's dream, enabling a rapist to overcome an intended victim's physical resistance and to discredit the victim's credibility as a witness against the rapist. Also, these drugs almost surely impede a rape survivor's recovery, though probably no studies have documented this. Likewise, little is written about how police, prosecutors and rape treatment centers should deal with the important evidentiary issues that arise when a victim has been administered Rohypnol, GHB or other date-rape drugs, and how to test for these drugs. . . .

Although little appears in the literature or case law, it is clear that far too many rapists know about and have access to these very dangerous date-rape drugs, and many of them are administering these drugs to their intended victims, particularly to women they know. Potentially this could impact many women, since about one in four women in America are raped during their lifetimes, and about three of four rapes in America are perpetrated by men who know their partners. While most known and suspected victims of these date-rape drugs are women, Rohypnol and GHB could also be effectively used against male and child victims.

What Is Rohypnol?

Rohypnol has never been legal to possess or manufacture in the United States. Simple possession of the drug in the United States is punishable by up to three years in prison as well as a fine. Under federal law, administering Rohypnol to another person without his or her knowledge and with intent to commit a crime of violence (including rape) is punishable by up to 20 years in prison and a fine. Distributing or importing one gram or more of Rohypnol is also punishable by up to 20 years in prison. In addition, a number of states (e.g., Idaho, Minnesota, New Mexico, North Dakota, Oklahoma and Pennsylvania) have placed Rohypnol under Schedule I control (even stiffer than under federal law), subjecting those possessing or distributing Rohypnol to state penalties as well.

Rohypnol can, however, be legally prescribed in 80 other countries where its use is recommended for the short-term treatment of severe sleep disorders. In fact, it is the most prescribed prescription sedative used in Europe. Since the late 1970's, abuse of Rohypnol has been reported in Europe, and more recently throughout the world. Rohypnol cannot be prescribed or legally sold in Canada, although it can be imported in limited amounts for personal use when prescribed by a foreign physician.

Rohypnol is the trade name for the central nervous system depressant drug, Flunitrazepam, a medication seven to ten times stronger than Valium and four to eight times stronger than Halcion, another drug from the benzodiazepine family (Xanax is another fairly well known member). It is legally manufactured in Mexico and several other countries by the Swiss-owned drug company, Hoffman-LaRoche, Inc., for sale outside of the United States. Because of Mexico's proximity to the United States and the ease in purchasing the drug over the counter in that country, virtually all of the supply that enters the United States comes through Mexico, primarily through Florida and Texas.

The Effects of Rohypnol

About 30 minutes after ingesting Rohypnol and, depending on the amount, for approximately the next eight hours, the drug causes muscle relaxation, slowing of psychomotor performance, lowered blood pressure, sleepiness, and often amnesia. "Some of the side effects" include "drowsiness, headaches, memory impairment, dizziness, nightmares, and tremors," according to an Office of National Drug Control Policy [ONDCP] Fact Sheet on Rohypnol (available by calling 1-800-666-3332). Long-term use often leads to physical dependence and the need for medically supervised withdrawal. Consumption of both Rohypnol and alcohol or other drugs can be deadly.

Rohypnol makes people ingesting it so weak or incapacitated or even unconscious that they are unable to resist a rapist or call out for help. They commonly experience difficulty in moving their arms or legs and their thinking is likely to be confused and impaired, with the result that they may appear to be drunk. Not only does Rohypnol slur a person's speech and make it difficult for the individual to walk, but the drug may impair the person's judgement or make the person less inhibited. Because of the drug's amnesia effects, a rape victim may be unable to remember what happened or who did it, and thus may be unable to identify the rapist or to even know she was sexually assaulted. Consequently, the victim may never call the police or rape crisis center to seek medical care. Also, any witness is likely to assume that the victim was drunk or consented to the attack since no protest or resistance is likely to have been observed. Rapists also like this drug because it is (at least until recently) tasteless, odorless and colorless, and easily dissolved in any liquid, so that it will not be detected, and the drug's fast-acting effects begin within minutes and last for many hours, typically peaking about two hours after ingestion.

Rohypnol's Use by Drug Users

Rohypnol is sometimes taken alone, and can be taken orally, snorted or injected. Drug users often take it with alcohol or marijuana to enhance their effects and use it to ease withdrawal symptoms of heroin, crack or cocaine. The drug usually costs less than $5 per tablet, making it affordable to those who abuse drugs. Although Hoffman-LaRoche sells it as a tablet in bubble packaging with a foil backing (making it look attractive and safe, as if it is legal medication), it is sometimes ground into a powder and on rare occasions may even be available in a liquid form. It is mainly used by younger people, who are often unaware of how dangerous it can be. The number of young people taking it have increased dramatically; in South Florida, the drug's main port of entry into the United States, it is estimated that the number of children who will take Rohypnol may soon equal the number who use marijuana.

On the street Rohypnol is known by many names, including circles, date-rape drug, dulcitas, forget me drug, forget pill, la rocha, lunch money drug (because of its low price), Mexican valium, mind erasers, minuses or negatives (referring to the 1 mg. tablet's markings) or pluses (the 2 mg. tablet's markings), pappas or potatoes (referring to the taker's mental capacity while under the influence), pingus, poor man's quaalude, R-2, reyrolds, rib, ro, roachies, roapies, robutal, rochas dos, roche, roofies, rope, rophies, rophy, ropies, roples, row-shay, ruvies, ruffles, trip-and-fall, or wolfies.

In response to the widespread misuse of Rohypnol, Hoffman-LaRoche recently added coloring to the tablets so that they will be more likely to be detected in clear fluids, and reformulated the tablets so that they will not dissolve as quickly in liquids. The drug manufacturing company is seeking approval for this new reformulation in the 80 countries where Rohypnol is legally marketed. The ONDCP Fact Sheet on Rohypnol notes that the new reformulated green colored Rohypnol "tablets can be detected in clear fluids and are visible in the bottom of a cup." Spiking a drink will prove more difficult, because the tablets will dissolve slowly.

GHB: Another Common Date-Rape Drug

Another drug affecting the central nervous system that is popular with rapists is Gamma-hydroxybutyrate, or GHB. While GHB has been tested in the United States for possible medical usage, it has never been approved for any such use. The claim that the drug enhances body building has never been clinically confirmed; while it can promote the secretion of growth hormones from the pituitary glands of healthy people, it has never been shown to promote the growth of muscles. The drug is very easy to concoct by heating a pot of gamma butyrolactone (a common industrial solvent) and adding sodium hydroxide and possibly acetone, ingredients readily available at most hardware stores and chemical supply houses.

Other names for GHB include bedtime scoop, cherry meth, easy lay, energy drink (to explain its saltiness), ever clear, G, gamma, Georgia home boy, G-juice, great hormones, grievous bodily harm (GBH), liquid E, liquid ecstasy, liquid sex, liquid soap, max (when dissolved in water and mixed with amphetamines), natural sleep 500, salt water, soap, sodium oxybate, scoop, somatomax PM, super-G, and water. . . .

GHB acts even faster than Rohypnol, its effects typically beginning 5–15 minutes after ingesting a dose, which is typically 1–2 teaspoons. Like Rohypnol, it can cause confusion, intense sleepiness, unconsciousness, dizziness, weakness, and memory loss. It can also cause nausea, vomiting, problems focusing the eyes, suppression of the gag reflex, hallucinations, uncontrollable twitching or tremors, seizures, heart and respiratory depression and coma, often requiring hospitalization. If its pH is too high (a fairly common result of home manufacture), GHB can also cause acid burns to the face, skin, and internal surfaces of anyone touching or ingesting the drug. When taken with alcohol or other drugs, the result can be fatal. Complicating the effects is the fact that most available GHB is concocted illegally by nondrug manufacturers, often with dangerous solvents and caustic soda mixed in, so that overdoses are all too common. The drowsiness

and weakness can last for up to three days, and the confusion for several weeks. Most symptoms last three to six hours. The body's mela-
tonin levels affect the drug's results, such that GHB is likely to have a
greater range of effects when taken at night, particularly in the winter,
than when taken during the daylight.

Although GHB appears to depress the central nervous system,
recent information from the Assistant State Attorney Robert Nichols of
the Broward County (FL) State Attorney's Office suggests that it may
actually over-excite it by stimulating the taker's brain waves, even into
seizure mode. It also has a tendency to exaggerate the feeling of intox-
ication, possibly causing the victim to feel enhanced sexual desire.
Such feelings, especially when they cause a victim to initiate or willingly participate in sexual activity, are almost certain to make the victim feel more guilty, depressed, and culpable. Curiously, the seriousness of the drug's effects are quickly forgotten, making drug abusers,
those administering it, and possibly even takers somewhat oblivious to
the drug's danger, thus increasing the risk for continued use.

Some of GHB's withdrawal symptoms include tremors, agitation,
paranoia, hallucinations, fevers, delirium, and seizures. The drug can
be psychologically addictive and has also caused a number of deaths.
The drug is made even more dangerous by the fact that a large dose is
needed to obtain the "desired" date-rape effects, though a relatively
small increase in dosage can result in severe damage or even death.

Most GHB is sold as a clear or syrupy liquid, although it is sometimes produced as a white powder that looks like white laundry
flakes. If in liquid form, a rapist can carry GHB in an eye or nose-
dropper bottle, and then administer a few squirts into the unwatched
glass of an intended victim. Drinks laced with GHB can sometimes be
detected because they often have an unpleasant, plastic, salty taste
and even a mild odor. However, it is not uncommon to mask the fla-
vor and smell by adding the drug to a sweet liqueur or fruit juice.

Considerations for Prosecutors

Rohypnol remains in the blood for only two to four hours after ingestion, can be detected in the blood for only two to four hours after
ingestion, but can be detected in urine for up to 72 hours, making
blood a far less reliable medium for testing. Hoffman-LaRoche will
test for the drug at no cost for law enforcement agencies, rape treatment centers and health care providers. GHB remains in the blood for
only four hours, and in the urine for at most 12 hours. Freezing or at
least refrigerating the samples will preserve them better for testing.
Victims who have been administered the most heavy doses of date-
rape drugs are far less likely to be able to seek medical or law enforcement attention in time to test positive, since the symptoms may last
for several days, and a severe hangover may follow.

Recently, hair has been successfully used to test for Rohypnol, although the first subjects tested were long-time abusers, who presumably have taken the drug in far greater concentrations. One advantage of hair testing is that it can be done long after the substance has disappeared from the blood and urine. For a date-rape victim, who presumably has only taken the drug once, detection will probably be more difficult.

It is not uncommon to find the bubble packs or other evidence of the drugs or their manufacture at the location of the scene of the crime or at the suspect's home. Bubble packs should be checked for the suspect's fingerprints, or for evidence of co-conspirators. Small containers that may have carried the drugs should be checked for residual amount of the substance. Similarly, evidence may show that the suspect used his computer for obtaining information about Rohypnol or GHB. Because it is not uncommon for drug-rapists to video or photograph their victims, such evidence or film receipts may implicate the suspect. . . .

Drug-rape crimes may be prosecuted at any of the following crime sites, some of which may be the same: (1) where the drug was manufactured; (2) where the victim was drugged; and (3) where the victim was raped or assaulted.

Possible crimes that can be charged when Rohypnol or GHB is used in connection with sexual assaults include sexual assault or rape, sexual assault of a mentally or physically incapacitated person, possession and delivery of a controlled substance, aggravated battery, and kidnapping. Additional charges may be appropriate when the victim is a minor. Because the administering of illegal drugs indicates premeditation, conspiracy crimes could also be charged, even if sexual assault does not happen.

A qualified toxicologist is probably needed to educate the jury about the effects of Rohypnol or GHB and to explain away apparent weaknesses in the case. The victim may have "voluntarily" consumed the drug or "consented" to sexual acts while under the influence. Unless the victim knew what was being administered and was aware of its effects, any apparent consent was not knowingly and freely given.

Remain Alert to the Dangers

The Rape Treatment Center, Santa Monica-UCLA Medical Center, released a series of well designed, informative brochures, posters and other materials, which can be used by rape crisis centers or campus programs to alert people to the dangers of Rohypnol, GHB and other "rape drugs." . . . [One] pamphlet wisely suggests that you not drink beverages that you did not personally open (e.g., drinks that have been passed around or poured from a punch bowl), that you left unattended, or that taste or look unusual (e.g., have a salty taste, excessive foam or strange residue or color). If you suspect you are being drugged, try to get help immediately by asking a friend for assistance, calling the police or getting medical help. Likewise, if a friend appears intoxicated, sick, passes out, has trouble breathing, or is otherwise acting strangely, call 911 for medical help. At a hospital emergency room, make them take a urine sample for testing at the state's crime lab (if they are able to test for date-rape drugs) or through Roche. Preserve all physical evidence possible by not urinating, showering, bathing, douching, or throwing away or laundering the clothes you were wearing during the incident. Save the drink or glass that held the drink if possible. And call a rape crisis center for information and support.

CHAPTER 2

WHAT CAUSES RAPE?

POWER IMBALANCES BETWEEN MEN AND WOMEN CONTRIBUTE TO RAPE

University of California-Davis Rape Prevention
Education Program

The University of California-Davis Rape Prevention Education Program (RPEP) is a component of the university's police department dedicated to reducing the incidence of sexual assault in the campus community. The following selection, an educational document drafted by the RPEP, outlines some of the sociological causes of rape. The authors of this document contend that the high rate of rape in the United States is largely the result of traditional sex roles that place women in subordinate positions in society. They maintain that women are vulnerable to sexual assault in part because they are conditioned to be passive, deferential, and unassertive with men. Such conditioning is rooted in a patriarchal, or male-ruled, culture that seeks to maintain men's dominance over women, the authors report.

Why does rape exist? What causes rape? What is it about our society that makes rape one of the fastest growing violent crimes in this country? Rape prevention techniques are very important in decreasing the vulnerability of individuals, but in order to eliminate the occurrence of rape from our society, we must first examine its causes more deeply so that we can take collective action. We must understand the sociology of rape in order to effectively work towards the elimination of it.

Despite the necessity for rape prevention, it is, to some degree, like applying a "band-aid" on the problem. The underlying reasons and causes for rape must be defined, examined and resolved or rape will not cease. Rape prevention must focus on eliminating the conditions in society which make women easy targets for rape. Victim control or rapist control alone are not effective. Victim control teaches women to avoid rape, but doesn't reduce the threat of rape. Furthermore, rape cannot always be avoided, no matter what precautions the woman

Excerpted from "Defining a Rape Culture," by the University of California-Davis Rape Prevention Education Program (http://pubweb.ucdavis.edu/Documents/RPEP/info.htm). Reprinted with permission from the University of California-Davis.

takes. It also puts part of the responsibility and blame for rape on the victim. Rapist control confuses prosecutions with prevention. There is little evidence that punishment serves as a deterrent. Besides, very few rapists are ever incarcerated.

From very early ages, men and women are conditioned to accept different roles. Women are raised to be passive and men are raised to be aggressive. We are conditioned to accept certain attitudes, values and behaviors. Our conditioning is continuously and relentlessly encouraged and reinforced by the popular media, cultural attitudes and the educational system. The media is a major contributor to gender-based attitudes and values. The media provides women with a complete list of behaviors that precipitate rape. Social training about what is proper and ladylike, as well as what is powerful and macho, teaches women to be victims and men to be aggressors.

The high incidence of rape in this country is a result of the power imbalance between men and women. Women are expected to assume a subordinate relationship to men. Consequently, rape can be seen as a logical extension of the typical interactions between women and men. One way to analyze the power relationship between men and women is by examining some of the common social rules women are taught.

Common "Social Rules" for Women

Rule #1: When spoken to, a woman must acknowledge the other person with a gracious smile.

Smiling and acknowledging almost any approach has become reflexive. For a potential rapist, this can serve as a "pretest" to determine how compliant a woman will be. Because women do not usually consider the option of ignoring an unwanted approach, they are more vulnerable. There are many reasons why women feel compelled to acknowledge someone they do not want to: peer group pressure; not wanting to hurt someone's feelings; women's lack of experience in acting on their own intuition about danger. The key to changing this comes in evaluating each approach as it comes and using your own feelings and needs as the main criteria for responding.

Rule #2: Women must answer questions asked of them.

In our culture, one of the rudest things a person can do is not answer a direct question. In social situations preceding rape, the man often puts the burden of rejection on the woman by asking questions such as, "What's wrong with you, don't you like me?" or, "What's wrong with you, don't you like men?" A woman often compensates for hurting the man's feelings by complying with his demands. It is important to consider each question you are asked against your own wishes at the moment.

Rule #3: Women must not bother other people or make a scene because they are uncomfortable.

Generally speaking, it is not ladylike to bother anyone at any time.

Women are not expected to intrude at any time, but rather, to be ready to help others at all times. When women scream for help, no one is willing to get involved. We have learned that yelling "FIRE" is much more effective than yelling "RAPE" or "HELP". Women are reluctant to draw attention to themselves, especially if in a place such as a party, bar, or dance. The solution is to solicit the help of others if a direct statement of "stop" is not heeded.

Rule #4: When in trouble, it is best to defer to the protection and judgment of men.

There are two flaws with this rule:

l) It is men who endanger or bother women, 2)there are not always trustworthy men around to protect women. Women must take the problem of victimization into their own hands; support and protect each other by being together, watching out for each other and understanding what it is like to be at the mercy of men.

Rule #5: Casual touching or suggestive comments in social settings are meant as a tribute to a woman's desirability.

Many women believe that being ogled by a group of construction workers is nothing more than a form of praise. Many sexual assaults, however, begin with a "harmless" compliment or inquiry from a rapist. His comments are a way of testing how accommodating the woman might be. The lack of clarity about what constitutes insulting behavior and the learned ambivalence women have about unwanted approaches makes them vulnerable to sexual assault.

Rule #6: It is the natural state of affairs for men to carry the financial burden of social situations.

This rule is losing some of its strength as more women are now paying their own way. This is still a popular rationale for men to justify demanding sex. The autonomy and self-respect that come with not always allowing an escort to pay is important in reacting to potentially dangerous situations.

Rule #7: When engaged in a social encounter, it is not proper for a woman to be superior in any game, sport or discussion if she wants to be accepted.

It has been held that beating a man at games, be it pool, tennis, scrabble, or monopoly, will hurt a man's pride and decrease his interest. It follows that if women are never allowed to win at anything with a man, it is expecting a great deal to ask a woman to effectively cope with a man who is trying to rape her. The danger in this is having a mind set that trivializes our own resources and talents in deference to a man's. This ridiculous unwritten rule of expected passivity needs to be recognized and eradicated in order for women to know they are capable of defending themselves.

Rule #8: Women should always accept and trust the kindness of strangers if they offer help.

Women tend to trust people who approach them or offer help. Unfortunately, the ploy of, "I'm helping you for your own good, you obviously need it," is used by potential rapists who have planned the crime in advance. The problem for women is that there is no way of knowing whether an overture of assistance is genuine or not. Therefore, it is best to limit the times where you might be in genuine need of help. Women must learn to scrutinize such "shoulds" more closely. Each individual woman must reexamine society's expectations of her. Once women have evaluated these rules of social behavior, they can create their own guidelines instead of adhering to, however unconsciously, these socially prescribed rules. . . .

Sexist Dictates

Women's vulnerability to rape is a result of their subordinate relationship to men. The set of beliefs and attitudes that divide people into classes by sex and justify one sex's superiority is called sexism. There are a number of sexist dictates that serve to maintain this subordinate relationship:

1. Women's status in society: Women occupy a relatively powerless position in society and are the recipients of fewer advantages and privileges. Men's benefits are built into a patriarchal system.
2. Rape as a means of control over women: Rape plays a role in maintaining patriarchy by perpetrating the threat of violence. The acts of just a few violent men can terrorize all women and can control women's lives. The indifference of other men reinforces this effect.
3. Women's dependence on men: Many women receive most of their benefits through men rather than through their own ability. This dependence is reinforced by the cultural belief that dependence is a "womanly" trait. Women are dependent on men for political representation, economic support, social position and psychological approval.

A strategy for eliminating women's vulnerability to rape involves altering the power relationship between women and men. Women's vulnerability will not end with individual change alone; there will have to be social change as well. The whole assumption of male superiority will have to be negated. Rape must be viewed as a political issue, because it keeps women powerless and reinforces the status quo of male domination.

Women's Socialization

The socialization of women must be changed. Society trains females to be physically and emotionally unequipped to respond effectively to danger. Training begins at an early age. Boys and girls are channeled into different physical activities because of the believed differences in physical and muscular development and stamina. Consequently, as adults, females are unable to gauge both their own bodies' resistance to injury and their own strength and power. Learning self-defense in schools and on the job would be a step towards alleviating women's vulnerability, as would providing girls and women with equal opportunities and encouragement to engage in sports. The emotional training women receive also contributes to their inability to successfully fight back. Women learn to be passive, gentle, nurturing, accepting and compliant. Rapists select victims they can intimidate and overpower. Most women are reluctant to challenge men's offensive behavior because of their emotional training and conditioning (i.e., it is not proper to "make a scene").

In addition, women tend to have an aversion to violence. It must be recognized that non-violence is no longer a virtue if it serves to maintain victimization. There is a difference between becoming a violent person and responding to violence in an appropriate and assertive manner. Women are not being encouraged to become violent individuals or to sanction violence, but rather to learn the skills to combat violent assaults against their persons.

Unfortunately, many women see themselves as powerless victims. Women can cultivate a confident and competent image. They need to learn direct and appropriate responses which reflect a seriousness about their refusal to be intimidated. Confrontation training helps women learn how to respond to men's suggestive and rude comments effectively.

Women are also kept vulnerable through their isolation from each other. Women are socialized to compete with each other for the attention of men and to mistrust each other. Collective strategies to eliminate rape must be utilized. Competition and mistrust are not conducive to collective strategizing among women. Women must learn to see other women as sources of aid and to work together to decrease the vulnerability of all women. It is important that women not blame themselves for the conditioning that has resulted in isolation.

The Problem of Isolation

Frequently, women psychologically distance themselves from the issue of rape and from each other by adopting the attitude that "It can't happen to me" or that "Only immoral women are raped." Community isolation also exists. Women within a community do not use and sometimes do not even see each other as resources. There are many factors which enforce the belief that "a woman's place is in the home." Consequently, women tend to be displaced from the mainstream of community action and decision making.

In order to deal with the problem of isolation, it is important to recognize and use the power of numbers. Women might develop ad-hoc committees, confrontation groups and support groups. More effective defenses can be planned by sharing common experiences and reactions to rape. Consciousness raising groups can work to identify and overcome sexist and racist attitudes. Through analysis of common problems, women can come to trust each other and recognize the effectiveness of their collective strength. Women can work in their neighborhoods to command public attention to their safety needs. . . .

Rape must be viewed as a political issue, not just another crime or mental health problem. It must be seen as an issue which affects all women. However, rape is not just a woman's problem—it is a community problem.

The Cultural Context of Date Rape

Py Bateman

Py Bateman has developed and produced a number of date rape prevention programs for teenagers and is the author of several educational booklets on adolescent sexuality. In the following essay, Bateman maintains that the problem of "date" rape—rape committed by a person the victim knows—is rooted in a culture that conditions boys to be sexually aggressive and girls to be passive. Such conditioning creates an environment that is conducive to rape, particularly during dating relationships in adolescence and young adulthood, Bateman points out. She concludes that establishing new courtship customs that emphasize equality and respect could help to prevent date rape among young people.

It has been estimated that over fifty percent of rapes are perpetrated against adolescents, with the vast majority taking place between individuals who know one another—that is, in an acquaintance or dating situation. Eugene Kanin, as early as 1957, reported that sixty-two percent of women surveyed had been victims of sexually aggressive acts during their last year of high school dating. In forty-four percent of those cases, the offender was either her steady boyfriend or fiancé. For twenty-one percent of those women, the sexually aggressive act was attempted or completed forced intercourse.

Twenty years later, in 1977, Kanin and Parcell found that eighty-three percent of college women respondents reported having been victims of sexual aggression, sixty-one percent since beginning college. Twenty-four percent of these cases involved forced intercourse. These early figures are not much different from the 1987 *Ms.* magazine study funded by the National Institute of Mental Health and conducted by Mary Koss. Koss questioned 6,159 students at thirty-two U.S. colleges and universities. One-quarter of the women surveyed reported having been victims of rape or attempted rape, eighty-four percent of them by acquaintances. Fifty-seven percent of the acquaintances were dates. In a 1984 study conducted by P. Levy, one out of ten young women interviewed stated that they had experienced forced sexual encounters while dating.

Condoning Sexual Violence

One of the major differences between the studies on courtship violence and those on date rape is that the former more frequently find similar rates of victimization for males and for females. Sexual aggression, however, remains an almost exclusively male province. In 1984, Sigelman, Berry, and Wiles, who included two items on sexual violence on their modified version of Straus's Conflict Tactics Scale, found only rare reports of female-committed sexual violence. More women reported having been victims of sexual aggression (thirty-five percent) than did men (twenty-one percent). In 1986, Makepeace found that eight times as many females as males felt they were victims of forced sex.

Such figures suggest that the problem of sexual abuse constitutes a cultural phenomenon and that survivors of such violence, according to Courtois, are the victims of "an endemic societal manifestation of the power imbalance between the sexes" where "men are conditioned into roles of power and dominance . . . and females . . . are conditioned to be passive and dependent." In other words, we live in a culture that condones sexual violence toward women.

Given this cultural context, it is not surprising that few young women report date rapes. Although accounts of the reporting rate for sexual assault vary, most investigators agree that reports by adolescent date rape victims are rare. Furthermore, many adolescents do not even recognize that a rape has occurred.

This lack of recognition may be a result of a remarkable tolerance for or justification of sexual assault when it is associated with dating or "romantic" involvement. In 1988, Miller reported that fifty-six percent of adolescent girls interviewed agreed that under certain circumstances, it is okay for the man to use force to obtain sex. In a 1987 study by Miller and Marshall, one of every six women interviewed reported that they believed that when a man became sexually aroused it was impossible to stop him or for him to stop himself. Twenty-seven percent of the young women interviewed said that they had engaged in unwanted sex because of psychological pressure from their boyfriends. They saw these experiences not as rape, but as part of "what happens on dates." A 1986 study by Fisher demonstrated that women with more traditional values are more accepting of forcible rape as well as less sure of what constitutes rape. It is evident that women in our culture are socialized to believe that satisfaction of a man's sexual urges is a woman's responsibility.

The Acceptability of Rape

Several studies indicate that men share in the belief that women are responsible for both stimulating and satisfying men's sexual urges, and that they hold other similar justifications for rape. In 1984, Malamuth attempted to determine the likelihood that men would rape if they could be assured of not being caught and punished. Across seven studies, an average of thirty-five percent of men indicated some likelihood that they would rape. In another study, Briere and Malamuth investigated both the likelihood to rape and the likelihood to use sexual force and found that sixty percent of male college students "indicated some likelihood of raping or using force in certain (albeit hypothetical) circumstances."

One might explain this self-reported likelihood of rape by noting that perhaps young men think of forced sexual intercourse in terms of being "masterful," imagining themselves to be Rhett Butler carrying Scarlett O'Hara up the stairs. As Lieutenant Samuels said to Cagney and Lacey in one episode of the so-named television series, "I can't understand why when Rhett Butler does it, it's romance, and when some guy on the street does it, it's rape."

It has been suggested that what is required is that young women learn to better communicate with young men in courtship situations. While improved communication will help, let us not excuse the offenders by blaming the victims for not saying what they mean. As Mary Beth Lacey replied to Samuels, "With all due respect, sir, if you can't tell the difference between romance and rape, you've got a problem."

Indeed, Kanin's 1967 study of male college students found that twenty-five percent admitted to physically forcing (or attempting to force) women to have sexual intercourse in situations in which the women responded by fighting or crying. Even if those women had not communicated more clearly, it takes a lot of distortion to interpret fighting or crying as consent.

So we see that not only do a significant number of young men think that rape is acceptable under some circumstances, and a majority report that they would force sexual intercourse if they knew they would not be caught, but a substantial minority admit to having committed sexual violence. These findings, and those describing the rate of physical violence in dating relationships, demand that we examine our culture, particularly our courtship customs, to discover the roots of this violence.

"Gatekeeper" Versus "Initiator"

It has been suggested by a number of authors that rape is a product of "overconformity" to masculinity. In 1985, Kanin reported that self-admitted date rapists reported greater peer pressure to be sexually active than nonrapists. He also documented the exploitive methods supported by peers that these rapists were likely to employ to force women to have sex. This suggests that the peer pressure to conform as a male may contribute to rape of intimates. It is also this aspect of courtship that makes it difficult for young men to set their own limits in their sexual exploration. The "custom" is that they must go as far as the girls will let them. The girls act as the "gatekeepers."

The source of this overconformity is that males are "supposed" to gain sexual experience, with a concentration on *quantity* rather than *quality*. Young men are not encouraged to consider the quality of the relationship in decision-making about sexual activity. It is the *doing* that is important. An example of this dilemma is evident in a problem that a boy brought to his high school counselor. He had gone out with a girl. As they were engaged in the sexual exploration common on dates, she told him to stop. He did. When he went to school, he heard from others that she had said that she did not mean for him to stop. She had expected him to push for more and was disappointed that he had not. He felt that he had "missed an opportunity." That feeling makes a lot of sense in the context of the male goal of "scoring." But if honesty and intimacy in relationships were the ideal, he would not feel disappointed, but relieved that he had withdrawn from sexual intimacy with someone who was not being honest.

The idea that "a real man doesn't take no for an answer" is related to the notion that "women don't mean it when they say no." If the boy does not initiate escalating sexual interaction until he is stopped by the girl in the gatekeeper role, he is seen as somehow falling short of the male ideal. The girl is caught between two ideals—one of the sexually reserved, "pure" madonna, the other of the sexually exciting "vamp" who can hold a boy's interest. She walks a fine line between being a "prude" and being a "slut." The opposing roles of initiator and gatekeeper set up an adversarial relationship in courtship. A belief that relationships between men and women are adversarial in nature is an attitude that has been linked to sexual aggression by authors Mary Koss and Kenneth Leonard, citing a number of different studies.

If "real ladies" don't say yes, and "real men" don't take no for an answer, then they must find another way to communicate. They attempt to send and interpret various "signals" of sexual availability. Unfortunately the sending and interpretation of these signals is anything but an efficient system of communication. We find males attempting to interpret female behavior in light of the question of sexual availability, sometimes with success, but often with a fair amount of confusion and distress.

College students, asked about their assumptions about young women's willingness to have sex, indicated that the following behavior led them to conclude that she was willing to have sexual intercourse: her initiating the date, allowing the man to pay for the date or going to the man's apartment. They were asked if it turned out that she definitely did not want sexual intercourse, he would be justified in forcing it. Rape was rated as justifiable by 27.5 percent of the men and 17.5 percent of the women. The leap between assuming willingness to have sex and justifying rape is understandable only in the context of the adversarial view of sexual relationships, shown to be common among sexually aggressive males, but not exclusive to them.

Adolescents often overcome conflicts inherent in the adversarial view of relationships by interacting in ways that allow the male perception of what is required to maintain the relationship to prevail. The expectation that men are "entitled" to have sex with their partners is consistent with the expectation that men dominate and maintain power and control over "their" women. The acceptance of this expectation is evident in the tendency of young men and women to see possessiveness and jealousy as demonstrating "love." They are then confused if the jealousy becomes abusive and if the expectation of the young man to maintain control is enforced with emotional, physical and sexual violence. Sexual intimacy in this context can be used as a form of punishment. It is a source of humiliation and shame for its victim, as she struggles with the expectations of her gatekeeper role and her role as the caretaker of the relationship and at the same time feels responsible for her own violation by a person she loves.

Preventing Date Rape

Given the depth of social support for sexually aggressive behavior among males, it is clear that those of us who work to prevent dating violence and/or serve its victims must offer an alternative to the current set of "courtship customs." As a long-term goal we can hope to offer young women and men a model of relationships built on equality and mutual respect and caring. Thus we can begin to build a social environment in which date rape and other forms of dating violence will stand out from the "norm." In the short-term, the description of this ideal should give young women the ability to recognize and avoid date rape. Such an ability, combined with the resources for both verbal and physical resistance, should result in a reduction of completed date rape. Likewise, the recognition and condemnation among young men of sexually aggressive behavior should also result in fewer attempts at date rape. A date rape prevention program must address equally these immediate needs of recognition and resistance and, at the same time, challenge the cultural context of dating violence.

THE EVOLUTIONARY BASIS OF RAPE

Randy Thornhill and Craig T. Palmer

For much of the past three decades, social scientists have argued that rape is motivated by hostility and violence rather than by sexual desire. In the following selection, scientists Randy Thornhill and Craig T. Palmer take issue with this theory, contending that rape is largely a sexually motivated crime. They assert that rape evolved as an alternative form of male reproductive behavior in insects, animals, and humans—particularly among species in which females are selective about their mates. Rape can help ensure that a male passes on his genes even when he is unable to secure willing sexual partners, the authors maintain. Thornhill is an evolutionary biologist at the University of New Mexico in Albuquerque. Palmer is an evolutionary anthropologist at the University of Colorado at Colorado Springs. They are the authors of A Natural History of Rape: Biological Bases of Sexual Coercion, from which the following article is adapted.

A friend of ours once told us about her rape. The details hardly matter, but in outline her story is numbingly familiar. After a movie she returned with her date to his car, which had been left in an isolated parking lot. She was expecting him to drive her home. Instead, the man locked the car doors and physically forced her to have sex with him.

Our friend was emotionally scarred by her experience: she became anxious about dating, and even about going out in public. She had trouble sleeping, eating and concentrating on her work. Indeed, like some war veterans, rape victims often suffer from post-traumatic stress disorder, in which symptoms such as anxiety, memory loss, obsessive thoughts and emotional numbness linger after a deeply disturbing experience. Yet gruesome ordeals like that of our friend are all too common: in a 1992 survey of American women aged eighteen and older, 13 percent of the respondents reported having been the victim of at least one rape, where rape was defined as unwelcome oral, anal or vaginal penetration achieved through the use or threat of force. Surely, eradicating sexual violence is an issue that modern society should make a top priority. But first a perplexing question must be

Reprinted from Randy Thornhill and Craig T. Palmer, "Why Men Rape," Sciences, January/February 2000. Adapted from their book A Natural History of Rape: Biological Bases of Sexual Coercion (Cambridge, MA: The MIT Press, 2000). Reprinted with permission from Randy Thornhill.

confronted and answered: Why do men rape?

The quest for the answer to that question has occupied the two of us collectively for more than forty years. As a purely scientific puzzle, the problem is hard enough. But it is further roiled by strong ideological currents. Many social theorists view rape not only as an ugly crime but as a symptom of an unhealthy society, in which men fear and disrespect women. In 1975 the feminist writer Susan Brownmiller asserted that rape is motivated not by lust but by the urge to control and dominate. In the twenty-plus years since, Brownmiller's view has become mainstream. All men feel sexual desire, the theory goes, but not all men rape. Rape is viewed as an unnatural behavior that has nothing to do with sex, and one that has no corollary in the animal world.

Undoubtedly, individual rapists may have a variety of motivations. A man may rape because, for instance, he wants to impress his friends by losing his virginity, or because he wants to avenge himself against a woman who has spurned him. But social scientists have not convincingly demonstrated that rapists are not at least partly motivated by sexual desire as well. Indeed, how could a rape take place at all without sexual motivation on the part of the rapist? Isn't sexual arousal of the rapist the one common factor in all rapes, including date rapes, rapes of children, rapes of women under anesthetic and even gang rapes committed by soldiers during war?

Rape Is a Sexual Act

We want to challenge the dearly held idea that rape is not about sex. We realize that our approach and our frankness will rankle some social scientists, including some serious and well-intentioned rape investigators. But many facts point to the conclusion that rape is, in its very essence, a sexual act. Furthermore, we argue, rape has evolved over millennia of human history, along with courtship, sexual attraction and other behaviors related to the production of offspring.

Consider the following facts:

- Most rape victims are women of childbearing age.
- In many cultures rape is treated as a crime against the victim's *husband*.
- Rape victims suffer *less* emotional distress when they are subjected to *more* violence.
- Rape takes place not only among human beings but also in a variety of other animal species.
- Married women and women of childbearing age experience more psychological distress after a rape than do girls, single women or women who are past menopause.

As bizarre as some of those facts may seem, they all make sense when rape is viewed as a natural, biological phenomenon that is a product of the human evolutionary heritage. Here we must hasten to emphasize that by categorizing a behavior as "natural" and "biological" we do not in any way mean to imply that the behavior is justified or even inevitable. *Biological* means "of or pertaining to life," so the word applies to every human feature and behavior. But to infer from that—as many of our critics assert that we do—that what is biological is somehow right or good, would be to fall into the so-called naturalistic fallacy. That mistake is obvious enough when one considers such natural disasters as epidemics, floods and tornadoes. In those cases it is clear that what is natural is not always desirable. And of course much can be, and is, done to protect people against natural threats—from administering antibiotics to drawing up emergency evacuation plans. In other words, the fact that rape is an ancient part of human nature in no way excuses the rapist.

Social Scientists Versus Evolutionists

Why, then, have the editors of scholarly journals refused to publish papers that treat rape from a Darwinian perspective? Why have pickets and audience protesters caused public lectures on the evolutionary basis of rape to be canceled or terminated? Why have investigators working to discover the evolutionary causes of rape been denied positions at universities?

The reason is the deep schism between many social scientists and investigators such as ourselves who are proponents of what is variously called sociobiology or evolutionary psychology. Social scientists regard culture—everything from eating habits to language—as an entirely human invention, one that develops arbitrarily. According to that view, the desires of men and women are learned behaviors. Rape takes place only when men learn to rape, and it can be eradicated simply by substituting new lessons. Sociobiologists, by contrast, emphasize that learned behavior, and indeed all culture, is the result of psychological adaptations that have evolved over long periods of time. Those adaptations, like all traits of individual human beings, have both genetic and environmental components. We fervently believe that, just as the leopard's spots and the giraffe's elongated neck are the result of aeons of past Darwinian selection, so also is rape.

That conclusion has profound and immediate practical consequences. The rape-prevention measures that are being taught to police officers, lawyers, parents, college students and potential rapists are based on the prevailing social-science view, and are therefore doomed to fail. The Darwinian theory of evolution by natural selection is the most powerful scientific theory that applies to living things. As long as efforts to prevent rape remain uninformed by that theory, they will continue to be handicapped by ideas about human nature that are fundamentally inadequate. We believe that only by acknowledging the evolutionary roots of rape can prevention tactics be devised that really work.

The Darwinian Perspective

From a Darwinian perspective, every kind of animal—whether grasshopper or gorilla, German or Ghanaian—has evolved to produce healthy children that will survive to pass along their parents' genetic legacy. The mechanics of the phenomenon are simple: animals born without traits that led to reproduction died out, whereas the ones that reproduced the most succeeded in conveying their genes to posterity. Crudely speaking, sex feels good because over evolutionary time the animals that liked having sex created more offspring than the animals that didn't.

As everyone knows all too well, however, sex and the social behaviors that go with it are endlessly complicated. Their mysterious and tangled permutations have inspired flights of literary genius throughout the ages, from *Oedipus Rex* to *Portnoy's Complaint*. And a quick perusal of the personal-growth section of any bookstore—past such titles as *Men Are from Mars, Women Are from Venus* and *You Just Don't Understand*—is enough to show that one reason sex is so complicated is that men and women perceive it so differently. Is that the case only because boys and girls receive different messages during their upbringing? Or, as we believe, do those differences between the sexes go deeper?

Over vast periods of evolutionary time, men and women have confronted quite different reproductive challenges. Whereas fathers can share the responsibilities of child rearing, they do not have to. Like most of their male counterparts in the rest of the animal kingdom, human males can reproduce successfully with a minimal expenditure of time and energy; once the brief act of sexual intercourse is completed, their contribution can cease. By contrast, the minimum effort required for a woman to reproduce successfully includes nine months of pregnancy and a painful childbirth. Typically, ancestral females also had to devote themselves to prolonged breast-feeding and many years of child care if they were to ensure the survival of their genes. In short, a man can have many children, with little inconvenience to himself; a woman can have only a few, and with great effort.

That difference is the key to understanding the origins of certain important adaptations—features that persist because they were favored by natural selection in the past. Given the low cost in time and energy that mating entails for the male, selection favored males who mated frequently. By contrast, selection favored females who gave careful consideration to their choice of a mate; that way, the high costs of mating for the female would be undertaken under circumstances that were most likely to produce healthy offspring. The result is that men show greater interest than women do in having a variety of sexual partners and in having casual sex without investment or commitment. That commonplace observation has been confirmed by many empirical studies. The evolutionary psychologist David M. Buss of the University of Texas at Austin, for instance, has found that women around the world use wealth, status and earning potential as major criteria in selecting a mate, and that they value those attributes in mates more than men do.

Remember, none of the foregoing behavioral manifestations of evolution need be conscious. People do not necessarily have sex because they want children, and they certainly do not conduct thorough cost-benefit analyses before taking a partner to bed. As Darwin made clear, individual organisms merely serve as the instruments of evolution. Men today find young women attractive because during human evolutionary history the males who preferred prepubescent girls or women too old to conceive were outreproduced by the males who were drawn to females of high reproductive potential. And women today prefer successful men because the females who passed on the most genes, and thereby became our ancestors, were the ones who carefully selected partners who could best support their offspring. That is why, as the anthropologist Donald Symons of the University of California, Santa Barbara, has observed, people everywhere understand sex as "something females have that males want."

The Frantic Quest for Sex

A dozen roses, romantic dinners by candlelight, a Tiffany engagement ring: the classic courtship ritual requires lots of time, energy and careful attention to detail. But people are far from unique in that regard: the males of most animal species spend much of their energies attracting, wooing and securing sexual partners. The male woodcock, for instance, performs a dramatic display each spring at mating time, soaring high into the air and then tumbling to the ground. Male fireflies are even flashier, blinking like neon signs. The male bowerbird builds a veritable honeymoon cottage: an intricate, sculpted nest that he decorates with flowers and other colorful bric-a-brac. Male deer and antelope lock antlers in a display of brute strength to compete for females.

Once a female's interest is piqued, the male behaves in various ways to make her more sexually receptive. Depending on the species, he dances, fans his feathers or offers gifts of food. In the nursery web spider, the food gift is an attempt to distract the female, who otherwise might literally devour her partner during the sex act. The common thread that binds nearly all animal species seems to be that males are willing to abandon all sense and decorum, even to risk their lives, in the frantic quest for sex.

But though most male animals expend a great deal of time and energy enticing females, forced copulation—rape—also occurs, at least occasionally, in a variety of insects, birds, fishes, reptiles, amphibians, marine mammals and nonhuman primates. In some animal species, moreover, rape is commonplace. In many scorpionfly species, for instance—insects that one of us (Thornhill) has studied in depth— males have two well-formulated strategies for mating. Either they offer the female a nuptial gift (a mass of hardened saliva they have produced, or a dead insect) or they chase a female and take her by force.

A remarkable feature of these scorpionflies is an appendage that seems specially designed for rape. Called the notal organ, it is a clamp on the top of the male's abdomen with which he can grab on to one of the female's forewings during mating, to prevent her escape. Besides rape, the notal organ does not appear to have any other function. For example, when the notal organs of males are experimentally covered with beeswax, to keep them from functioning, the males cannot rape. Such males still mate successfully, however, when they are allowed to present nuptial gifts to females. And other experiments have shown that the notal organ is not an adaptation for transferring sperm: in unforced mating, the organ contributes nothing to insemination.

Not surprisingly, females prefer voluntary mating to mating by force: they will approach a male bearing a nuptial gift and flee a male that does not have one. Intriguingly, however, the males, too, seem to prefer a consensual arrangement: they rape only when they cannot obtain a nuptial gift. Experiments have shown that when male scorpionflies possessing nuptial gifts are removed from an area, giftless males—typically, the wimpier ones that had failed in male-male competitions over prey—quickly shift from attempting rape to guarding a gift that has been left untended. That preference for consensual sex makes sense in evolutionary terms, because when females are willing, males are much more likely to achieve penetration and sperm transfer.

Human males obviously have no external organ specifically designed for rape. One must therefore look to the male psyche—to a potential mental rape organ—to discover any special-purpose adaptation of the human male to rape.

Male Sexual Strategies

Since women are choosy, men have been selected for finding a way to be chosen. One way to do that is to possess traits that women prefer: men with symmetrical body features are attractive to women, presumably because such features are a sign of health. A second way that men can gain access to women is by defeating other men in fights or other kinds of competitions—thereby gaining power, resources and social status, other qualities that women find attractive.

Rape can be understood as a third kind of sexual strategy: one more way to gain access to females. There are several mechanisms by which such a strategy could function. For example, men might resort to rape when they are socially disenfranchised, and thus unable to gain access to women through looks, wealth or status. Alternatively, men could have evolved to practice rape when the costs seem low—when, for instance, a woman is alone and unprotected (and thus retaliation seems unlikely), or when they have physical control over a woman (and so cannot be injured by her). Over evolutionary time, some men may have succeeded in passing on their genes through rape, thus perpetuating the behavior. It is also possible, however, that rape evolved not as a reproductive strategy in itself but merely as a side effect of other adaptations, such as the strong male sex drive and the male desire to mate with a variety of women.

Take, for instance, the fact that men are able to maintain sexual arousal and copulate with unwilling women. That ability invites inquiry, according to the psychologist Margo Wilson of McMaster University in Hamilton, Ontario, and her coworkers, because it is not a trait that is common to the males of all animal species. Its existence in human males could signal that they have evolved psychological mechanisms that specifically enable them to engage in forced copulation—in short, it could be a rape adaptation. But that is not the only plausible explanation. The psychologist Neil M. Malamuth of the University of California, Los Angeles, points out that the ability to copulate with unwilling women may be simply a by-product of men's "greater capacity for impersonal sex."

Explaining the Persistence of Rape

More research is needed to decide the question of whether rape is an adaptation or merely a by-product of other sexual adaptations. Both hypotheses are plausible: one of us (Thornhill) supports the former, whereas the other (Palmer) endorses the latter. Regardless of which hypothesis prevails, however, there is no doubt that rape has evolutionary—and thus genetic—origins. All traits and behaviors stem from a complex interplay between genes and the environment. If rape is an adaptation, men must possess genes that exist specifically because rape increased reproductive success. If rape turns out to be merely a side effect of other adaptations, then the genes involved exist for reasons that have nothing to do with rape. Either way, however, the evolutionary perspective explains a number of otherwise puzzling facts about the persistence of rape among human males.

For example, if rape is evolutionary in origin, it should be a threat mostly to women of childbearing age. And, in fact, young adult women are vastly overrepresented among rape victims in the female population as a whole, and female children and post-reproductive-age women are greatly underrepresented.

By the same token, if rape has persisted in the human population through the action of sexual selection, rapists should not seriously injure their victims—the rapist's reproductive success would be hampered, after all, if he killed his victim or inflicted so much harm that the potential pregnancy was compromised. Once again, the evolutionary logic seems to predict reality. Rapists seldom engage in gratuitous violence; instead, they usually limit themselves to the force required to subdue or control their victims. A survey by one of us (Palmer), of volunteers at rape crisis centers, found that only 15 percent of the victims whom the volunteers had encountered reported having been beaten in excess of what was needed to accomplish the rape. And in a 1979 study of 1,401 rape victims, a team led by the sociologist Thomas W. McCahill found that most of the victims reported being pushed or held, but that acts of gratuitous violence, such as beating, slapping or choking, were reported in only a minority of the rapes—22 percent or less. A very small number of rape victims are murdered: about .01 percent (that figure includes unreported as well as reported rapes). Even in those few cases, it may be that the murder takes place not because the rapist is motivated by a desire to kill, but because by removing the only witness to the crime he greatly increases his chance of escaping punishment

Emotional Pain as a Defense Mechanism

Rape is more distressing for women than are other violent crimes, and evolutionary theory can help explain that as well. In recent years research on human unhappiness informed by evolutionary theory has developed substantial evidence about the functional role of psychological pain. Such pain is thought to be an adaptation that helps people guard against circumstances that reduce their reproductive success; it does so by spurring behavioral changes aimed at preventing future pain. Thus one would expect the greatest psychological pain to be associated with events that lower one's reproductive success, and, indeed, emotionally traumatic events such as the death of a relative, the loss of social status, desertion by one's mate and the trauma of being raped can all be interpreted as having that effect.

Rape reduces female reproductive success in several ways. For one thing, the victim may be injured. Moreover, if she becomes pregnant, she is deprived of her chance to choose the best father for her children. A rape may also cause a woman to lose the investment of her long-term partner, because it calls into question whether the child she later bears is really his. A variety of studies have shown that both men and women care more for their genetic offspring than for stepchildren.

One of us (Thornhill), in association with the anthropologist Nancy W. Thornhill, has conducted a series of studies on the factors that contribute to the emotional pain that women experience after a rape. Those studies confirmed that the more the rape interfered with the women's reproductive interests, the more pain they felt. The data, obtained from the Joseph J. Peters Institute in Philadelphia, came from interviews with 790 girls and women who had reported a sexual assault and who were subsequently examined at Philadelphia General Hospital between 1973 and 1975. The subjects, who ranged in age from two months to eighty-eight years, were asked a variety of questions designed to evaluate their psychological responses to the rape. Among other things, they were asked about changes in their sleeping habits, in their feelings toward known and unknown men, in their sexual relations with their partners (children were not asked about sexual matters), and in their eating habits and social activities.

Analysis of the data showed that young women suffered greater distress after a rape than did children or women who were past reproductive age. That finding makes evolutionary sense, because it is young women who were at risk of being impregnated by an undesirable mate. Married women, moreover, were more traumatized than unmarried women, and they were more likely to feel that their future had been harmed by the rape. That, too, makes evolutionary sense, because the doubt a rape sows about paternity can lead a long-term mate to withdraw his support.

Among the women in the study, psychological pain rose inversely to the violence of the attack. In other words, when the rapist exerted less force, the victim was more upset afterward. Those findings, surprising at first, make sense in the evolutionary context: a victim who exhibits physical evidence that sexual access was forced may have less difficulty convincing her husband or boyfriend that what took place was rape rather than consensual sex. In evolutionary terms, such evidence would be reassuring to a pair-bonded male, because rape is a one-time event, whereas consensual sex with other partners is likely to be frequent, and thus more threatening to paternity.

Finally, women of reproductive age reported more emotional distress when the assault involved sexual intercourse than when it involved other kinds of sexual behavior. Among young girls and older women, however, penile-vaginal intercourse was no more upsetting than other kinds of assaults. Again, the possibility of an unwanted pregnancy may be a key factor in the degree of trauma the victim experiences.

For all those reasons, the psychological pain that rape victims suffer appears to be an evolved defense against rape. The human females who outreproduced others—and thus became our ancestors—were people who were highly distressed about rape. Their distress presumably served their interests by motivating them to identify the circumstances that resulted in the rape, assess the problems the rape caused, and act to avoid rapes in the future.

Rape Education

If women today are to protect themselves from rape, and men are to desist from it, people must be given advice that is based on knowledge. Insisting that rape is not about sex misinforms both men and women about the motivations behind rape—a dangerous error that not only hinders prevention efforts but may actually *increase* the incidence of rape.

What we envision is an evolutionarily informed program for young men that teaches them to restrain their sexual behavior. Completion of such a course might be required, say, before a young man is granted a driver's license. The program might start by inducing the young men to acknowledge the power of their sexual impulses, and then explaining why human males have evolved in that way. The young men should learn that past Darwinian selection is the reason that a man can get an erection just by looking at a photo of a naked woman, why he may be tempted to demand sex even if he knows that his date truly doesn't want it, and why he may mistake a woman's friendly comment or tight blouse as an invitation to sex. Most of all, the program should stress that a man's evolved sexual desires offer him no excuse whatsoever for raping a woman, and that if he understands and resists those desires, he may be able to prevent their manifestation in sexually coercive behavior. The criminal penalties for rape should also be discussed in detail.

Young women also need a new kind of education. For example, in today's rape-prevention handbooks, women are often told that sexual attractiveness does not influence rapists. That is emphatically not true. Because a woman is considered most attractive when her fertility is at its peak, from her mid-teens through her twenties, tactics that focus on protecting women in those age groups will be most effective in reducing the overall frequency of rape.

Young women should be informed that, during the evolution of human sexuality, the existence of female choice has favored men who are quickly aroused by signals of a female's willingness to grant sexual access. Furthermore, women need to realize that, because selection favored males who had many mates, men tend to read signals of acceptance into a woman's actions even when no such signals are intended.

In spite of protestations to the contrary, women should also be advised that the way they dress can put them at risk. In the past, most discussions of female appearance in the context of rape have, entirely unfairly, asserted that a victim's dress and behavior should affect the degree of punishment meted out to the rapist: thus if the victim was dressed provocatively, she "had it coming to her"—and the rapist would get off lightly. But current attempts to avoid blaming the victim have led to false propaganda that dress and behavior have little or no influence on a woman's chances of being raped. As a consequence, important knowledge about how to avoid dangerous circumstances is often suppressed. Surely the point that no woman's behavior gives a man the right to rape her can be made without encouraging women to overlook the role they themselves may be playing in compromising their safety.

Until relatively recently in Europe and the United States, strict social taboos kept young men and women from spending unsupervised time together, and in many other countries young women are still kept cloistered away from men. Such physical barriers are understandably abhorrent to many people, since they greatly limit the freedom of women. But the toppling of those barriers in modern Western countries raises problems of its own. The common practice of unsupervised dating in cars and private homes, which is often accompanied by the consumption of alcohol, has placed young women in environments that are conducive to rape to an extent that is probably unparalleled in history. After studying the data on the risk factors for rape, the sex investigators Elizabeth R. Allgeier and Albert R. Allgeier, both of Bowling Green State University in Ohio, recommended that men and women interact only in public places during the early stages of their relationships—or, at least, that women exert more control than they generally do over the circumstances in which they consent to be alone with men.

An evolutionary perspective on rape might not only help prevent rapes but also lead to more effective counseling for rape victims. A therapy program explaining that men rape because they collectively want to dominate women will not help a victim understand why her attacker appeared to be sexually motivated, why she can no longer concentrate enough to conduct her life effectively, or why her husband or boyfriend may view the attack as an instance of infidelity. In addition, men who are made aware of the evolutionary reasons for their suspicions about their wives' or girlfriends' claims of rape should be in a better position to change their reactions to such claims.

Ideology Versus Knowledge

Unlike many other contentious social issues, such as abortion and homosexual rights, everyone has the same goal regarding rape: to end it. Evolutionary biology provides clear information that society can use to achieve that goal. Social science, by contrast, promotes erroneous solutions, because it fails to recognize that Darwinian selection has shaped not only human bodies but human psychology, learning patterns and behavior as well. The fact is that men, relative to women, are more aggressive, sexually assertive and eager to copulate, and less discriminating about mates—traits that contribute to the existence of rape. When social scientists mistakenly assert that socialization alone causes those gender differences, they ignore the fact that the same differences also exist in all the other animal species in which males offer less parental investment than females and compete for access to females.

In addressing the question of rape, the choice between the politically constructed answers of social science and the evidentiary answers of evolutionary biology is essentially a choice between ideology and knowledge. As scientists who would like to see rape eradicated from human life, we sincerely hope that truth will prevail.

RAPE IS NOT A NATURAL ACT

Laura Flanders

In their book *A Natural History of Rape*, scientists Randy Thorn-hill and Craig Palmer claim that rape is a result of evolution—a natural by-product of the male reproductive drive. In the follow-ing selection, Laura Flanders disagrees with this theory, arguing that Thornhill and Palmer rely on insufficient data to draw their conclusions and ignore information that contradicts their ideas. For example, Flanders points out, Thornhill and Palmer fail to explain how male-on-male rape or the rape of elderly women could result from innate reproductive incentives. Moreover, she writes, the two scientists seem to be more interested in criticizing sociological explanations for rape than in providing a plausible theory about the cause of rape. Flanders is a contributing editor of *In These Times*, a biweekly newsmagazine.

All men are natural-born rapists. This is not the sort of allegation that usually gets serious treatment in the mainstream media. But Randy Thornhill and Craig T. Palmer have been journalistically feted from coast to coast for making just that charge. The attention has been enough to more than double the print-run of their book, *A Natural History of Rape*, three months before its March 2000 release by the Massachusetts Institute of Technology. Not bad for a couple of uncharismatic guys with a meandering theory based on bug research. The key to their success: They use their theory to criticize not rapists, but feminists.

Professors of evolutionary biology at the University of New Mexico and evolutionary anthropology at the University of Colorado, respec-tively, Thornhill and Palmer argue that rape has given rapists a repro-ductive edge in the contest for genetic selection. Rape may be hard-wired into the species. At the very least, it is a product of the male breeding drive.

Darwin to the Rescue?

While the writers say rape is wrong and that they are out to stop it, they contend we need to face facts. For a quarter of a century, they

Reprinted from Laura Flanders, "Natural Born Rapists," *In These Times*, March 6, 2000. Reprinted with permission from *In These Times*.

say, people informed by Susan Brownmiller's *Against Our Will* have viewed rape as "unnatural behavior having nothing to do with sex." That hasn't worked. But where feminists have failed, Darwin can come to the rescue.

Heaven forbid. The techniques these guys propose to stop rape sound like suggestive counseling. Just in case a young man's thoughts have not naturally drifted to sexual violence, Thornhill and Palmer advise lecturing boys on the "impulses" that are their birthright. And they caution young women that because evolution has favored men who are quickly aroused, "the way they dress can put them at risk."

But in the excerpt that appears in the January/February 2000 edition of *The Sciences*, Thornhill and Palmer provide no data to back up the claim that the skimpily dressed are raped more often than the frumpy. Instead, much is made of a grabbing appendage on scorpionflies (insects Thornhill has studied in depth) that seems to suggest that the natural world designs for better raping. The authors point to data that they say show that most rape is not "gratuitously" violent, that most raped women are of child-bearing age, and that the most "distressed" rape victims are fertile and married. But the studies they cite are 20 years old—done before a movement helped survivors to talk openly. Clearly their sources (absent in the abstract) deserve a closer look.

Sloppy Science

"It's advocacy and the science is sloppy," says Jerry Coyne, an evolutionary biologist at the University of Chicago. This is not the first time Thornhill has been accused of sloppy science. A few years back, *Time* dedicated its cover to a Thornhill "report" linking symmetrical features to genetic health and better sex. That too, was based on dubious data. But Coyne says half the reporters he has spoken to seem to have only the slightest idea of Thornhill and Palmer's thesis. "They've mostly read other media accounts," he says.

Indeed, the media have swept the two from the dry world of science journalism to the country's most popular talk shows. *Dateline* and *Today* interviewers have swallowed their science whole. The way Melinda Penkava introduced Thornhill on National Public Radio's *Talk of the Nation* was typical: "Now evolutionary science enters the picture." "Scientist" Thornhill was put up against "feminist" Brownmiller.

And that's the point. There is no original research in "Why Men Rape," and their theory ignores a multitude of contradictions. Stumped by homosexual rape, the rape of the old and the young, and by the impotence of many rapists, Thornhill and Palmer simply ignore assaults that make no reproductive sense. But even they know better. In an essay he co-authored in 1983, Thornhill was honest enough to point to a contemporary estimate that only "about 50 percent of rapes include ejaculation." He ignores that here.

Biology Versus Sociology

What Thornhill and Palmer are really about is advancing the cause of biology against sociology. "This is the *Bell Curve* of anti-feminism," says Jackson Katz, creator of a new film from the Media Education Foundation, *Tough Guise: Violence, Media and the Crisis of Masculinity.* [*The Bell Curve* is a 1994 book that argues that different races have different intellectual abilities.] "It discourages tackling the economic, social and political factors that support male violence."

As Coyne—a biologist himself—puts it, "They're on a mission to swallow up social studies." That's why the first chapter of their book is dedicated not to rape, but to an attack on social scientists, who, they say, mistakenly over-emphasize social learning. "In reality, every aspect of every living thing is by definition biological," they write.

Well, sure. We live and breathe with quirky equipment developed over generations. But thinking and choosing and wanting and hating are hard things to explain in a laboratory.

Thornhill and Palmer aren't the first to consider that maybe all men are potential rapists. Rape survivors often grapple with that thought. It occurred to Karen Pomer, who was raped in 1995 by a man who went on to rape an 83-year-old woman. But years of work on sexual violence led her to a different conclusion: "I don't think people do this if something didn't happen to them," she says. "I'm glad we're asking why men rape, but 'because it's natural' is no sort of answer."

PORNOGRAPHY AS A CAUSE OF RAPE

Diana E.H. Russell

Feminist researcher Diana E.H. Russell is professor emerita of sociology at Mills College in Oakland, California. She has written and edited several books on sexual violence against women and children. In the following selection, Russell presents evidence revealing that exposure to pornography can provoke some men to rape. She maintains that pornography often portrays women as enjoying being brutalized and raped. Although pornography is not the sole cause of sexual violence, Russell contends, it can significantly undermine male inhibitions against committing rape and should be considered an important factor in the persistence of the problem of rape.

When addressing the question of whether or not pornography causes rape, as well as other forms of sexual assault and violence, many people fail to acknowledge that the actual *making* of pornography sometimes involves, or even requires, violence and sexual assault. Testimony by women and men involved in such activity provides numerous examples of this.

In one case, a man who said he had participated in over a hundred pornographic movies testified at the 1986 Attorney General's Commission hearings in Los Angeles as follows:

> I, myself, have been on a couple of sets where the young ladies have been forced to do even anal sex scenes with a guy which *[sic]* is rather large and I have seen them crying in pain.

Another witness gave the following testimony at the same hearings in Los Angeles:

> Women and young girls were tortured and suffered permanent physical injuries to answer publisher demands for photographs depicting sadomasochistic abuse. When the torturer/photographer inquired of the publisher as to the types of depictions that would sell, the torturer/photographer was instructed to get similar existing publications and use the depiction therein for instruction. The torturer/photographer

followed the publisher's instructions, tortured women and girls accordingly, and then sold the photographs to the publisher. The photographs were included in magazines sold nationally in pornographic outlets. . . .

It should not be assumed that violence occurs only in the making of violent pornography. For example, although many people would classify the movie *Deep Throat* as nonviolent pornography because it does not portray rape or other violence, we now know from Linda (Lovelace) Marchiano's two books, as well as from her public testimony, that this film is, in fact, a documentary of her rape from beginning to end.

Most people, including some of the foremost researchers on pornography in the United States, ignore the violence used by pornographers in the manufacturing of these misogynist materials. As Catharine MacKinnon points out . . ., pornography is somebody's life before it becomes the pornographer's free speech. Testimony presented at the hearings held on the antipornography civil rights ordinance in Minneapolis, Minnesota, in 1983 provides powerful evidence for the truth of her statement.

Before we can address the issue of pornography as a cause of rape, it is important to know the proclivities of those who read and view pornography. Hence, data on males' propensity to rape will be presented next.

Males' Propensity to Rape

> Why do I want to rape women? Because I am basically, as a male, a predator and all women look to men like prey. I fantasize about the expression on a woman's face when I "capture" her and she realizes she cannot escape. It's like I won, I own her.

> —Male respondent quoted in Shere Hite's 1981 book *The Hite Report on Male Sexuality.*

Research indicates that 25% to 30% of male college students in the United States and Canada admit that there is some likelihood they would rape a woman if they could get away with it. In the first study of males' self-reported likelihood to rape that was conducted at the University of California at Los Angeles, the word *rape* was not used; instead, an account of rape (described below) was read to the male subjects, of whom 53% said there was some likelihood that they would behave in the same fashion as the man described in the story *if* they could be sure of getting away with it. Without this assurance, only 17% said they might emulate the rapist's behavior. It is pertinent to know exactly what behavior these students said they might emulate:

> Bill soon caught up with Susan and offered to escort her to her

car. Susan politely refused him. Bill was enraged by the rejection. "Who the hell does this bitch think she is, turning me down," Bill thought to himself as he reached into his pocket and took out a Swiss army knife. With his left hand he placed the knife at her throat. "If you try to get away, I'll cut you," said Bill. Susan nodded her head, her eyes wild with terror.

The story then depicted the rape. There was a description of sexual acts with the victim continuously portrayed as clearly opposing the assault.

In another study, 356 male students were asked:

If you could be assured that no one would know and that you could in no way be punished for engaging in the following acts, how likely, if at all, would you be to commit such acts?

Among the sexual acts listed were the two of interest to these researchers: "forcing a female to do something she really didn't want to do" and "rape." *Sixty percent of the sample indicated that under the right circumstances, there was some likelihood that they would rape, use force, or do both.* . . .

Some people dismiss the findings from these studies as "merely attitudinal." However, this conclusion is incorrect. Neil Malamuth has found that male subjects' self-reported likelihood of raping is correlated with physiological measures of sexual arousal to rape depictions. Clearly, erections cannot be considered attitudes.

More specifically, the male students who say they might rape a woman if they could get away with it are significantly more likely than other male students to be sexually aroused by portrayals of rape. Indeed, these males were more sexually aroused by depictions of rape than by mutually consenting depictions. In addition, when asked if they would find committing a rape sexually arousing, they said yes. They were also more likely than the other male subjects to admit to having used actual physical force to obtain sex with a woman. These latter data were self-reported, but because they refer to actual behavior, they too cannot be dismissed as merely attitudinal.

Looking at the sexual arousal data alone (as measured by penile tumescence) rather than its correlation with self-reported likelihood to rape, Malamuth reports that:

- About 10% of the population of male students is sexually aroused by "very extreme violence" with "a great deal of blood and gore" that "has very little of the sexual element."
- About 20% to 30% show substantial sexual arousal by depictions of rape in which the woman never shows signs of arousal, only abhorrence.
- About 50% to 60% show some degree of sexual arousal by a rape

depiction in which the victim is portrayed as becoming sexually aroused at the end.

Given these findings, it is hardly surprising that after reviewing a whole series of related experiments, Neil Malamuth concluded that "the overall pattern of the data is . . . consistent with contentions that many men have a proclivity to rape.". . .

The Meaning of "Cause"

Smoking is not the only cause of lung cancer; nor is pornography the only cause of rape. I believe there are many factors that play a causal role in this crime. I will not attempt to evaluate the relative importance of different causal factors in this essay, but merely to show the overwhelming evidence that pornography is a major one of them.

Because all viewers of pornography are not equally affected by it, many people conclude that pornography cannot be playing a causative role in rape and other forms of violence against women. This is similar to the tobacco industry's defense of cigarette smoking. They maintain that because many smokers do not die of lung cancer, and because some nonsmokers *do* die of this disease, it is incorrect to believe that smoking causes lung cancer. But the tobacco industry's reasoning here is faulty. They have no grounds for assuming that the proponents of smoking as a cause of lung cancer believe that smoking is the *only* cause. . . .

In my 1984 book *Sexual Exploitation,* I suggest many factors that may predispose a large number of males in the United States to want to rape or assault women sexually. Some examples discussed in that book are (a) biological factors, (b) childhood experiences of sexual abuse, (c) male sex-role socialization, (d) exposure to mass media that encourage rape, and (e) exposure to pornography. Here I will discuss only the role of pornography.

Although women have been known to rape both males and females, males are by far the predominant perpetrators of sexual assault as well as the biggest consumers of pornography. Hence, my theory will focus on male perpetrators. . . .

Given the intense debate about whether or not pornography plays a causal role in rape, it is surprising that so few of those engaged in it ever state what they mean by "cause." A definition of the concept of *simple causation,* according to George Theodorson and Achilles Theodorson, follows:

> An event (or events) that precedes and results in the occurrence of another event. Whenever the first event (the cause) occurs, the second event (the effect) necessarily or inevitably follows. Moreover, in simple causation the second event does not occur unless the first event has occurred. Thus the cause is both the SUFFICIENT CONDITION and the NECESSARY CONDITION for the occurrence of the effect.

By this definition, pornography clearly does not cause rape, as it seems safe to assume that some pornography consumers do not rape women and that many rapes are unrelated to pornography. However, the concept of *multiple causation* (defined below by Theodorson and Theodorson) *is* applicable to the relationship between pornography and rape.

> With the conception of MULTIPLE CAUSATION, various possible causes may be seen for a given event, any one of which may be a sufficient but not necessary condition for the occurrence of the effect, or a necessary but not sufficient condition. In the case of multiple causation, then, the given effect may occur in the absence of all but one of the possible sufficient but not necessary causes; and, conversely, the given effect would not follow the occurrence of some but not all of the various necessary but not sufficient causes.

As I have already presented the research on males' proclivity to rape, I will next discuss some of the evidence that pornography can be a sufficient (though not a *necessary*) condition for males to desire to rape. . . .

Pornography Undermines Inhibitions Against Rape

Evidence has already been cited showing that 25% to 30% of males admit that there is some likelihood that they would rape a woman if they could be assured that they would get away with it. It is reasonable to assume that a substantially higher percentage of males would *like* to rape a woman but would refrain from doing so because of their internal inhibitions against these coercive acts. Presumably, the strength of these males' motivation to rape as well as their internal inhibitions against raping range from very weak to very strong, and also fluctuate in the same individual over time.

There are several ways in which pornography can undermine some males' internal inhibitions against acting out rape desires. . . .

1. Objectifying Women. Feminists have been emphasizing the role of objectification (treating females as sex objects) in the occurrence of rape for many years. Males' tendency to objectify females makes it easier for them to rape girls and women. James Check and Ted Guloien note that other psychologists have observed that "dehumanization of victims is an important disinhibitor of cruelty toward others." The rapists quoted in the following passages demonstrate the link between objectification and rape behavior.

> It was difficult for me to admit that I was dealing with a human being when I was talking to a woman, because, if you read men's magazines, you hear about your stereo, your car, your chick.

After this rapist had hit his victim several times in her face, she stopped resisting and begged him not to hurt her.

> When she said that, all of a sudden it came into my head, "My God, this is a human being!" I came to my senses and saw that I was hurting this person.

Another rapist said of his victim, "I wanted this beautiful fine *thing* and I got it."

Dehumanizing oppressed groups or enemy nations in times of war is an important mechanism for facilitating brutal behavior toward members of those groups. Ms. U, for example, testified that

> A society that sells books, movies, and video games like "Custer's Last Stand [Revenge]" on its street corners, gives white men permission to do what they did to me. Like they [her rapists] said, I'm scum. It is a game to track me down, rape and torture me.

The dehumanization of women that occurs in pornography is often not recognized because of its sexual guise and its pervasiveness. It is also important to note that the objectification of women is as common in nonviolent pornography as it is in violent pornography. . . .

Some Men Believe Women Enjoy Rape

2. Rape Myths. If males believe that women enjoy rape and find it sexually exciting, this belief is likely to undermine the inhibitions of some of those who would like to rape women. Sociologists Diana Scully and Martha Burt have reported that rapists are particularly apt to believe rape myths. Scully, for example, found that 65% of the rapists in her study believed that "women cause their own rape by the way they act and the clothes they wear"; and 69% agreed that "most men accused of rape are really innocent." However, as Scully points out, it is not possible to know if their beliefs preceded their behavior or constitute an attempt to rationalize it. Hence, findings from the experimental data are more telling for our purposes than these interviews with rapists.

Since the myth that women enjoy rape is widely held, the argument that consumers of pornography realize that such portrayals are false is totally unconvincing. Indeed, several studies have shown that portrayals of women enjoying rape and other kinds of sexual violence can lead to increased acceptance of rape myths in both males and females. In an experiment conducted by Neil Malamuth and James Check, for example, one group of college students saw a pornographic depiction in which a woman was portrayed as sexually aroused by sexual violence, and a second group was exposed to control materials. Subsequently, all subjects were shown a second rape portrayal. The students who had been exposed to the pornographic depiction of rape were significantly more likely than the students in the control group:

1. to perceive the second rape victim as suffering less trauma;
2. to believe that she actually enjoyed being raped; and
3. to believe that women in general enjoy rape and forced sexual acts.

Other examples of the rape myths that male subjects in these studies are more apt to believe after viewing pornography are as follows:

- A woman who goes to the home or the apartment of a man on their first date implies that she is willing to have sex;
- Any healthy woman can successfully resist a rapist if she really wants to;
- Many women have an unconscious wish to be raped, and may then unconsciously set up a situation in which they are likely to be attacked;
- If a girl engages in necking or petting and she lets things get out of hand, it is her own fault if her partner forces sex on her.

In Kristin Maxwell and James Check's 1992 study of 247 high school students, they found very high rates of what they called "rape supportive beliefs," that is, acceptance of rape myths and violence against women. The boys who were the most frequent consumers of pornography, who reported learning a lot from it, or both, were more accepting of rape supportive beliefs than their peers who were less frequent consumers of pornography and/or who said they had not learned as much from it.

A quarter of girls and 57% of boys expressed the belief that it was at least "maybe okay" for a boy to hold a girl down and force her to have intercourse in one or more of the situations described by the researchers. In addition, only 21% of the boys and 57% of the girls believed that forced intercourse was "definitely not okay" in any of the situations. The situation in which forced intercourse was most accepted was when the girl had sexually excited her date. In this case, 43% of the boys and 16% of the girls stated that it was at least "maybe okay" for the boy to force intercourse on her.

According to Edward Donnerstein, "After only 10 minutes of exposure to aggressive pornography, particularly material in which women are shown being aggressed against, you find male subjects are much more willing to accept these particular [rape] myths." These males are also more inclined to believe that 25% of the women they know would enjoy being raped.

3. Acceptance of Interpersonal Violence. Males' internal inhibitions against acting out their desire to rape can also be undermined if they consider male violence against women to be acceptable behavior. Studies have shown that when male subjects view portrayals of sexual violence that have positive consequences—as they often do in pornography—it increases their acceptance of violence against women. Examples of some of the beliefs used to measure acceptance of interpersonal violence include the following:

- Being roughed up is sexually stimulating to many women;
- Sometimes the only way a man can get a cold woman turned on is to use force;
- Many times a woman will pretend she doesn't want to have intercourse because she doesn't want to seem loose, but she's really hoping the man will force her.

Malamuth and Check conducted an experiment of particular interest because the movies shown were part of the regular campus film program. Students were randomly assigned to view either a feature-length film that portrayed violence against women as being justifiable and having positive consequences *(Swept Away* or *The Getaway)* or a film without sexual violence. Malamuth and Check found that exposure to the sexually violent movies increased the male subjects' acceptance of interpersonal violence against women, but not the female subjects' acceptance of this variable. These effects were measured several days after the films had been seen. . . .

Downplaying the Problem of Rape

4. Trivializing Rape. According to Donnerstein, in most studies on the effects of pornography, "subjects have been exposed to only a few minutes of pornographic material." In contrast, Dolf Zillmann and Jennings Bryant examined the impact on male subjects of what they refer to as "massive exposure" to nonviolent pornography (4 hours and 48 minutes per week over a period of 6 weeks). After 3 weeks the subjects were told that they were participating in an American Bar Association study that required them to evaluate a trial in which a man was prosecuted for the rape of a female hitchhiker. At the end of this mock trial, various measures were taken of the subjects' opinions about the trial and about rape in general. For example, they were asked to recommend the prison term they thought most fair.

Zillmann and Bryant found that the male subjects who had been exposed to the massive amounts of pornography considered rape a less serious crime than they had before they were exposed to it; they thought that prison sentences for rape should be shorter; and they perceived sexual aggression and abuse as causing less suffering for the victims, even in the case of an adult male having sexual intercourse with a 12-year-old girl. The researchers concluded that "heavy exposure to common nonviolent pornography trivialized rape as a criminal offense."

The more trivialized rape is in the perceptions of males who would like to rape women or girls, the more likely they are to act out their desires. Since the research cited above shows that exposure to pornography increases males' trivialization of rape, it is reasonable to infer that this process contributes to undermining some male consumers' internal inhibitions against acting out their desires to rape. . . .

5. Acceptance of Male Dominance in Intimate Relationships. A marked increase in males' acceptance of male dominance in intimate relationships was yet another result of the massive exposure to pornography. The notion that women are, or ought to be, equal in intimate relationships was more likely to be abandoned by these male subjects. Finally, their support of the women's liberation movement also declined sharply.

These findings demonstrate that pornography increases the acceptability of sexism. As Van White points out, "by using pornography, by looking at other human beings as a lower form of life, they [the pornographers] are perpetuating the same kind of hatred that brings racism to society."

For example, Ms. O testified about the ex-husband of a woman friend and next-door neighbor: "When he looked at the magazines, he made hateful, obscene, violent remarks about women in general and about me. He told me that because I am female I am here to be used and abused by him, and that because he is a male he is the master and I am his slave."

Rapists as a group reveal a higher acceptance of male dominance in intimate relationships than nonrapists. Since Zillmann and Bryant's research shows that exposure to pornography increases males' acceptance of male dominance in intimate relationships, it is reasonable to infer that this process contributes to undermining some male consumers' internal inhibitions against acting out their desires to rape.

6. *Desensitizing Males to Rape.* In an experiment specifically designed to study desensitization, Donnerstein and Daniel Linz showed 10 hours of R-rated or X-rated movies over a period of 5 days to male subjects. Some students saw X-rated movies depicting sexual assault; others saw X-rated movies depicting only consenting sex; and a third group saw R-rated sexually violent movies—for example, *I Spit on Your Grave, Toolbox Murders,* and *Texas Chainsaw Massacre.* Donnerstein describes *Toolbox Murders* as follows:

> There is an erotic bathtub scene in which a woman massages herself. A beautiful song is played. Then a psychotic killer enters with a nail gun. The music stops. He chases the woman around the room, then shoots her through the stomach with the nail gun. She falls across a chair. The song comes back on as he puts the nail gun to her forehead and blows her brains out.

According to Donnerstein, many young males become sexually aroused by this movie.

Donnerstein and Linz described the impact of the R-rated movies on their subjects as follows:

> Initially, after the first day of viewing, the men rated themselves as significantly above the norm for depression, anxiety, and annoyance on a mood adjective checklist. After each subsequent day of viewing, these scores dropped until, on the

fourth day of viewing, the males' levels of anxiety, depression, and annoyance were indistinguishable from baseline norms.

By the fifth day, the subjects rated the movies as less graphic and less gory and estimated fewer violent or offensive scenes than after the first day of viewing. They also rated the films as significantly less debasing and degrading to women, more humorous, and more enjoyable, and reported a greater willingness to see this type of film again. Their sexual arousal to this material, however, did not decrease over this 5-day period.

On the last day, the subjects went to a law school, where they saw a documentary reenactment of a real rape trial. A control group of subjects who had never seen the films also participated in this part of the experiment. Subjects who had seen the R-rated movies: (a) rated the rape victim as significantly more worthless, (b) rated her injury as significantly less severe, and (c) assigned greater blame to her for being raped than did the subjects who had not seen the films. In contrast, these effects were not observed for the X-rated nonviolent films. However, the results were much the same for the violent X-rated films, despite the fact that the R-rated material was "much more graphically violent."

Donnerstein and Linz point out that critics of media violence research believe "that only those who are *already* predisposed toward violence are influenced by exposure to media violence." This view is contradicted by the fact that Donnerstein and Linz actually preselected their subjects to ensure that they were not psychotic, hostile, or anxious; that is, they were not predisposed toward violence prior to the research.

Donnerstein and Linz's research shows that exposure to woman-slashing films (soft-core snuff pornography) increases males' desensitization to extreme portrayals of violence against women. It seems reasonable to infer that desensitization contributes to undermining some male viewers' internal inhibitions against acting out their desires to rape.

In summary: I have presented only a small portion of the research evidence for several different effects of pornography, all of which probably contribute to the undermining of some males' internal inhibitions against acting out their rape desires. This list is not intended to be comprehensive. . . .

Some people argue that because there is some unknown number of men who have consumed pornography but who have never raped a woman, the theory that porn can cause rape is thereby disproven. This is comparable to arguing that because some cigarette smokers don't die of lung disease, there cannot be a causal relationship between smoking and lung cancer. Only members of the tobacco industry and some seriously addicted smokers consider this a valid argument today.

CHAPTER 3

RAPE'S AFTERMATH

Contemporary Issues
Companion

RAPE CHANGES A WOMAN'S LIFE

Liza N. Burby

Women who have been raped often travel down a long and difficult road to recovery, reports Liza N. Burby in the following
selection. Initially, she explains, many rape victims experience
the symptoms of post-traumatic stress disorder: fear, flashbacks
of the attack, sleeplessness, excessive vigilance, and shame. Even
several years after the rape, victims might still be plagued by
frightening memories of the assault and often encounter difficulties with intimate relationships, Burby maintains. According to
the author, the best thing that a concerned friend or family
member can do for a rape victim is to listen to her story and
remain patient during the healing process. Burby is a frequent
contributor to *Newsday*, a New York City area periodical.

On a summer night in 1981, Patricia Weaver Francisco awoke from a
deep sleep to terror in the dark. There was a stranger in her bedroom.
Before she could even blink, the man leapt on her and raped her.
When he left, he took with him treasured items from her jewelry
box—and her very faith in life.

She was 30 years old.

In the immediacy of her trauma, there was no way she could imagine the laborious passage she would face to recovery—or that it would
take 15 years.

Nearly 18 million American women have been raped, according to a
1998 National Violence Against Women survey, funded by the Departments of Justice and Health and Human Services. It's not likely that
they will forget the anniversary of the crime. At "You Are Not Alone: A
Day Honoring Women Who Have Survived Rape and Those Who Have
Given Them Voice" in Los Angeles, nearly 500 women from around
the country stood up one by one to announce their dates. One of
them, a teenager, had been raped only seven weeks earlier; another
woman listed three dates, according to Karen Pomer, co-coordinator of
the Rainbow Sisters Project, which organized the event. The group is
making plans for a similar gathering, perhaps in Manhattan.

Despite the record nationwide decline in crime, including rape, announced by the FBI, one in seven women will be raped during her lifetime, according to the Justice Department. Many of them will need a decade or more to come to terms with it. Some never will fully. For 65 percent, post-traumatic stress syndrome will make it difficult to function at work or school, with family or friends.

During the first days and weeks after being raped, women typically experience hypervigilance, anger, fear, guilt, tearfulness and shame, says Lori Pietrafesa, a social worker at Family Counseling Associates in Garden City. As they struggle to resume normal life, many experience flashbacks, particularly during moments of physical intimacy. They may avoid sex altogether, have insomnia and headaches, and they may develop phobias, such as the fear of going outside alone.

Francisco was surprised at how many stages and how many years she needed to recover. "I remember a nurse in the hospital telling me it would take three years before my life would come back, and I told her she was crazy, that I didn't even have three weeks for this. I didn't ask for it, and I didn't want to devote any time to it. It was an arrogant reaction. I had no idea I had so far to go," says Francisco, the Minneapolis-based author of "Telling: A Memoir of Rape and Recovery" (Cliff Street Books, $23).

As Francisco experienced, rape causes a woman to lose trust in the world, says Elizabeth Carll, a Centerport resident and author of "Violence in Our Lives: Impact on Workplace, Home and Community" (Allyn and Bacon, $29.99). This is even more likely if she knew the man. Unlike the image of a rapist lurking behind the bushes, 78 percent of rapes are not perpetrated by strangers. But women are less likely to feel responsible if the rapist is someone they don't know. And women who know the rapist are more affected by shame.

"So they are not as likely to talk about it and are less likely to get help. Only 5 percent of rapes are reported," Carll says. "But unless you share it, you tend to think you're the only one this happened to. When you talk to others, suddenly it's easier not to assume that blame."

Recovery can also depend on prior experiences. For instance, women who were sexually abused as children have a more powerful reaction to rape, says Roberta Graziano, associate professor at the Hunter College School of Social Work in Manhattan and a Flushing resident.

Other factors include the degree of violence in the assault, the woman's social support and her age, says Pietrafesa. "For an adolescent, the rape may be her first sexual experience, and because she is still developing her sense of ego she is more likely to have a longer healing period," she explains. "When a woman is more mature, she usually has that ego strength and support system in place to help her. Also, teens may suppress their feelings for years, only to have them resurface."

Teens are often reluctant to tell anyone, because they feel humiliated or fear their parents will take away privileges. A 28-year-old woman from Dix Hills recalls not wanting her parents to know that she was raped at a party while others looked on. She was 16 and a virgin.

"It took awhile for it to affect me," says the woman, who did not want her name published. "I was so confused at first—because I thought that sex equals love—that I called him up and actually talked to him. Then I went through a period in which I didn't want to be touched. I cried on dates. I started to have flashbacks that I wasn't sure were real, because while they seemed realistic they were more horrifying than I remember the experience being."

She regrets that she didn't tell her parents, because it meant she never got help. "It actually took me 10 years to get to a place where I finally felt I had control over intimate situations and to start accepting my body, and until a couple of years ago to finally enjoy sex," she says.

For a South Shore woman, parental support was key. She was a senior in high school when she was kidnaped and raped three times by two men as she was leaving her after-school job. While other girls were worrying about their prom dresses and dates, she was talking to police and prosecutors and identifying her attackers.

Almost two decades later, she says she cringes more than most people do over violent images, and ideas of bondage and torture make her nauseous. "I have no anger," she says, "but I do have a superhero/martyr complex I'm trying to work through. I also have deep-rooted feelings of entitlement because I was a victim. It's one of the reasons my marriage broke up. I've gone through bouts of depression that are usually set off by the anniversary date or man problems."

Indeed, the most adversely affected part of a rape survivor's life is usually her relationship with a partner—with most marriages ending.

"But unless the husband is blaming and unsupportive, this is not about his inadequacies. It's about what she brings into the room with her," says Graziano. "It's hard for someone who was assaulted to feel she can be with someone who will not hurt her. You'll have to expect that sex will be affected for a long time."

Francisco's husband saw her through strained sexual relations, wild anger and crippling fears that left her unable to walk from her car to her front door, all for many years. Just when they thought she was finally doing better, the difficult childbirth of their son sent her right back to square one. Thirteen years after she was assaulted, their marriage ended.

"I remember him saying to me a couple of years after the rape, `When are you coming back? This is getting hard.' I knew then I was never coming back, that the person I had been before the rape was dead, and I grieved for her and was so angry that the person I had been was gone," she says. "It's tragic for the person who loves you and has to come to know you now. It's a terrible position for a partner to be in."

Graziano says that after time for healing, relationships may work better for those who were raped before meeting their partner.

Deborah Gellis, 38, of Flushing, was sexually abused as a child and raped in two separate incidents as an adolescent. She had been in treatment for alcohol abuse—which she says was a direct result of her experiences—when she met Barrie, her husband of 13 years.

Barrie, 49, says Deborah told him her story on their first date and soon after they went to couples' therapy together. "We spent a lot of time talking about it and working together to learn how to deal with her moods when they came up," he says. "As a partner, you shouldn't blame the person who was raped. You're on the same side."

Deborah says: "It took a tremendous amount of work. Sometimes he'd just lift his hand, and I'd duck. I'd have flashbacks during sex. It took years and years of slow healing wounds. It takes a strong person to deal with their spouse's reactions."

A woman who has been raped may be overprotective of her children, daughters in particular, says Graziano—although some women may not be vigilant enough, because they don't believe they will be able to protect their child. Childbirth can also be traumatic. Graziano recommends that a pregnant woman tell her physician what happened so they can work together to make her feel safe about the birth experience.

It helps to recognize that the healing process can be lengthy, Pietrafesa says. "Sometimes . . . the reaction of people around you is that you're lucky to be alive, so you should be over it by now. Sympathy wears off more quickly than the survivor needs."

"It helps to know you're reacting normally to an abnormal situation. You'll only create more problems for yourself if you bury or deny your feelings," says Gary Dunn, chief psychiatrist at South Nassau Communities Hospital Counseling Center in Baldwin.

It helps to have your partner involved in treatment in some way, Pietrafesa adds, and to channel your anxieties into a constructive activity, such as political activism about rape. The Gellises created an award-winning video for public-access TV, "The Naked Truth on Incest." The South Shore woman turned her experience into inspiration to work in the system to help other victims and became a prosecutor. The Dix Hills woman volunteered to speak about her experience in a date-rape program. "As I spoke, I saw recognition and sadness on so many faces in the group. Kids came up to me after and spoke about their experiences, and I felt a huge burden fall off my shoulders," she says. "Even though I had more to do, I believe that was an important part of my healing process. Just the fact that someone else knows even remotely what you experienced helps, because you feel so alone when rape happens to you."

It helps to attend a support group, Francisco found. "Recovery is something you can't do alone," she says. "Rape is very powerful. But that power can eventually be used to transform your life. You can come through it to have a happy life." On the 10-year anniversary of her attack, she sat down to begin her book.

The Family's Role: Listen, Be Patient

If your wife, daughter, sister or friend is raped, life as all of you knew it is suddenly changed, says Patricia Weaver Francisco, a rape survivor who has written about her experience. Helping your loved one through the long healing process and the wide-ranging symptoms of post-traumatic stress syndrome can be emotionally draining and confusing.

The best thing you can do is listen to what the rape survivor has to say, Francisco says. If hearing the story makes you uncomfortable, acknowledge that, rather than risk reacting in such a way that makes her ashamed of what she's telling you.

Patience—in large doses—will be important, Francisco says, because the process of healing can go on for a long time, with unsettling reactions such as flashbacks in moments of intimacy and startling fears of affectionate gestures or shadows. "Do your best to accept her reality rather than talk her out of it, which would prove fruitless and frustrating for both of you," she advises. "For instance, don't tell her to 'snap out of it' or to 'get over it already.'"

Be open to the inevitable changes her trauma will cause for you, as you become more vigilant about safety, for instance. "To say this won't change your life is to resist her natural healing process as well as your own," Francisco says.

Remember that, even though the powerful emotion of shame affects not only the survivor of rape but also family members, the disgrace belongs only to the perpetrator, Francisco says. And remember that although you're likely to feel guilty that you weren't able to protect her—particularly if you're the parent of a young victim—the rapist alone is responsible for what happened.

It's normal to feel both outraged and helpless if your child has been raped, but any anger should be directed at the rapist—not your child, says Joanne Gorman, sexual assault response coordinator for the Victims Information Bureau in Hauppauge. You will undoubtedly be more anxious about your child's safety, as well as that of other family members, but recognize that this is normal and be patient with yourself.

Gorman advises all family members of a person who has been raped to seek counseling, either from an individual therapist or a support group, in order to talk about their feelings—including concerns about how difficult it is to help a rape survivor heal.

HELPING THE WOUNDS HEAL

Mimi Callaghan

In the following selection, Mimi Callaghan encourages all victims of rape and sexual abuse to seek immediate help. Stranger rape, date rape and incest are all traumatic, she points out, and victims of such abuse need to talk with someone they can trust to help them deal with feelings of anxiety, shame, and depression. Rape survivors who participate in counseling or group therapy can eventually heal from the wounds inflicted by sexual violence, the author maintains. Callaghan was a student at Edward R. Murrow High School in New York City when she wrote this piece for *New Youth Connections*, a monthly magazine written by and for New York youth.

Survivors of rape often do not know how to handle their feelings about what has happened to them. Victims should know that there are people out there who want to help them. Patti Feuereisen is a psychologist who counsels teenage girls who have been raped or sexually abused. She had a lot of information and advice to offer.

First of all, she said, a rape victim should go straight to a hospital after the attack. Most hospitals have a rape crisis unit. Hospitals also have counselors who can help rape victims deal with their feelings.

Talking It Out

Dr. Feuereisen said it is extremely important to talk to someone, whether it is a counselor, a best friend or a parent. Talking about what happened can help victims deal with their feelings of terror, shame and humiliation.

"Rape survivors have different reactions. Some girls go into denial, they make themselves believe that nothing happened to them. They block it out. Now this can be very dangerous," said Dr. Feuereisen. "They could have a delayed reaction about a year or more later when something reminds them of what happened."

Many people who have been raped believe they will never get over the trauma. But Dr. Feuereisen said that teenagers who have been raped and who talk out their feelings can expect to feel happy about their lives again within a few years.

Reprinted from Mimi Callaghan, "Recovering from Rape: Helping the Wounds Heal," *New Youth Connections*, April 1998. Copyright © 1998 Youth Communication, 224 W. 29th St., 2nd Floor, New York, NY 10001. Reprinted with permission from New Youth Connections.

Some people believe that one type of rape, either date rape or rape by a stranger, is more traumatic than the other. This is completely untrue, Dr. Feuereisen said. Each is a violation and has its own trauma and problems.

In cases of date rape, the girl often feels responsible or guilty. Victims of date rape may blame themselves for being drunk or high, or they may feel like they led the guy on by being flirtatious. But these things never make a date rape a girl's fault.

Girls Should Band Together

If a girl feels guilty, she often doesn't want to talk about it or deal with what happened. Sometimes date rape victims even stay with the guy. But it is important for all victims of rape to talk about it and get support.

Dr. Feuereisen also suggested that when girls go to parties, they take steps to decrease their chances of getting raped.

They shouldn't be drunk or stoned alone. If they want to get some play, that's fine, but girls should make it clear where their limits are. For the guy, getting some play might be going all the way.

"Girls need to band together and watch out for one another; guys will not defend girls. If you're going to get drunk and stoned, make sure you have a friend who is clean that is going to be looking out for you," Dr. Feuereisen said.

Anxiety and Panic

When a girl is raped by a stranger, she tends to feels less guilty and she is more likely to go to counseling.

Stranger rape causes girls to feel anxiety and panic states in everyday life. They are often scared of the subways, they have nightmares and tremors, and they're afraid to go outside.

Girls who have been raped can have trouble sleeping, and they can get so depressed they eat too much or not at all. Eating disorders may develop. Often their grades take a dive.

Guys can be raped, too, and sometimes it can be harder for them to admit it, because they think rape only happens to girls.

But if a guy is raped, he needs help, too.

Victims of incest should also seek help. Kids who have been sexually abused suffer from many of the same problems as rape victims, Dr. Feuereisen said.

And incest can be even more traumatic, because an older person whom you trust is victimizing you.

"Sometimes when a girl is younger and she is molested, later on in life she doesn't know how to say no to sex. Incest survivors often become promiscuous. This could affect her throughout her adult life," Dr. Feuereisen said.

In Dr. Feuereisen's opinion, a girl who has been raped or sexually abused should see a female counselor and should receive interactive counseling, where the girl and the counselor both talk.

"Survivors should not be afraid to talk about what happened. Sometimes they are afraid or ashamed and some are scared to relive the incident, but some have to relive it every day. It is OK to think all these things," Dr. Feuereisen

She also recommended group therapy. That way the girls know that they are not alone.

She suggested that victims should be open with what happened to them because it will make it easier for them later on.

However, she warned that they will probably get some negative criticism from people who don't understand what happened. In cases of date rape especially, some people will say you deserved it somehow.

Girls also have to realize that being raped or molested might affect future relationships. Girls may feel afraid to trust a partner and may fear physical pain during intercourse.

Rape victims have trouble feeling comfortable or being able to get excited by physical intimacy. This is because the body can shut off natural responses that happen during intimacy. Dr. Feuereisen said it takes time and work, but victims will get over it and get back to normal.

A Wound That Will Heal

"I see rape as a scar or wound that has just been cut open," Dr. Feuereisen said. "When it opens, it is vulnerable. When it is sewn up it takes a long time for the flesh to heal. You can always feel the scar, always feel something. You will feel it less and less even though you know it is always there. But you will get over it."

BEYOND BROKEN PROMISES

Joseph J. Guido

Nationally, 20 to 25 percent of college women claim that they were sexually assaulted during their student career, reports Joseph J. Guido in the following selection. These women usually know their attackers, he points out, but most do not report the assault, nor do they confide in parents, therapists, or counselors. This is unfortunate, Guido contends, because women often experience debilitating emotional distress after a rape. University counselors and other concerned individuals need to become more aware of the warning signs that indicate that a student may have been raped. The opportunity to tell the story of one's assault and to be part of a supportive community is critical to healing, the author maintains. Guido, a Catholic priest, is a psychologist for the Personal Counseling Center at Providence College in Rhode Island.

As the nation's colleges and universities begin a new academic year and students and their parents arrive on campus in minivans packed with the trappings of college life, the talk is of hope and promise and dreams, and rightly so. It is a time when faculty and students are eager to return to the classroom, when new friends are made and old friendships renewed and when parents have the bittersweet experience of saying goodbye to the children they have raised while marveling at the young men and women they have become. The late summer journey from home to campus is a kind of American pilgrimage, and, like all pilgrimages, it is sustained by a prayer for safety, grace and final success.

Sexual Assault at College

Unfortunately, for some this prayer will seem to go unanswered as the dream of the new school year becomes a nightmare because of sexual assault. Nationally 20 to 25 percent of college women report that they were sexually assaulted while students. This means that of those fresh-faced 18-year-olds who arrive on campus for the first time this September, as many as one in four will be fondled against her will or forced to perform sexual acts or raped in the course of her college career. The assailant typically will not be a stranger but a boyfriend, friend or acquaintance, and most likely she will not be assaulted in some remote or dangerous setting but in the familiar surroundings of a dorm room, at an off-campus party or when friends are close by. Almost always alcohol or drugs or both will be involved. She will probably never report her assault to college or university officials or the police, and it is unlikely that she will confide in her parents, her advisor, a campus minister or counselor. She may tell selected friends, but most often she will keep it to herself, attempting to go on alone and in silence as if the promise with which college began had never been betrayed.

But a betrayal has taken place, and its consequences are real. Although the effects of sexual assault vary and no individual experiences them all, young women commonly experience depression and anxiety in its wake, are prone to self-doubt and blame, can develop difficulties eating, studying and sleeping, and often use alcohol and drugs to numb the pain. The lucky ones have strong and supportive families and avail themselves of the help available through this channel. Those less fortunate or more seriously affected can become self-destructive, either literally or symbolically, and can be plagued by disabling memories and reminiscences of the assault.

Although nothing can undo the fact of the assault, healing can take place if the silence and isolation can be breached. Research suggests that the opportunity to tell the story of one's assault and to be part of a supportive community are critical to healing. Although this is in part a task for therapists, it is also the responsibility of the wider community of the family, campus and church. Indeed, the natural therapy of human love and relationship—and purposeful engagement with contexts of meaning and value that transcend the individual and a particular moment in time—have the capacity to sustain and enrich one who has been assaulted long after the important but modest goals of counseling have been achieved.

The question then becomes how to provide the conditions for healing. Drawing on my own experience as a priest and psychologist who has worked with college students for 17 years, I suggest that we can ask them about their experience, listen and believe what we hear, be more willing to follow than to lead the students' healing and serve as a bridge between their shaken faith and the steady grace of God.

Students have told me repeatedly that no one asked them whether they had been assaulted, even though there was every indication that something had gone drastically wrong. Warning signs like a precipitous decline in grades, abrupt changes in mood or personality, the sloughing off of old friends and the acquisition of new and troubling acquaintances, the abuse of alcohol or drugs, an aversion to dating or alternately engaging in promiscuous behavior may have been met with worry and solicitous concern, and even generous offers of help. But these indicators rarely elicit an inquiry about sexual assault, and often, therefore, the concern is to little effect.

Shame and Denial

The failure to ask about sexual assault is not for want of good intentions, but it may collude with a student's own shame and inhibition. Many students who have been sexually assaulted feel ashamed and fault themselves. "I was stupid," "I was flirting," "I had been drinking," "I should have known better," "I am weak," "I should have yelled or called for help or fought him off," are common refrains even among those who would never blame others in similar circumstances. Added to this is the peculiar nature of student culture. With respect to campus authorities, students often abide by an implicit code of silence that effectively protects the guilty and penalizes victims who name names. At the same time, rampant gossip about the intimate details of one another's lives leaves students vulnerable to distortions and misperceptions about their person and character against which they have no appeal. Our silence can therefore unwittingly reinforce that of a woman already confused about her responsibility and hemmed in by the culture of her peers.

Asking about sexual assault is like asking about suicide—difficult in any event but harder to do in anticipation than in fact. Simply put and stated with the reason for concern, the question can challenge the rule of silence and give permission for what needs to be said. It should not be the first or only question to be asked, nor should it be asked by everyone of every student in difficulty, but it is a question to be asked when suspicions are aroused. And if asked judiciously and in a timely and appropriate manner, it can be a first step in healing. But by asking about sexual assault we are also committing ourselves to listen and to believe what we hear.

One student told me that when she first told her parents that she had been assaulted, her mother responded, "No you weren't." Although we might be inclined to attribute this reaction to shock, the reports of other students suggest that it is an extreme example of a common tendency to deny the reality of sexual assault. For some students, the initial relief at having told someone is followed by disappointment and confusion when the assault is never referred to again, as if having been disclosed it should be over and done with, life can go on and one must forgive and forget. Still others summon the courage to file a formal complaint against their assailant only to find that it is they who are effectively on trial or that the system that promised to protect or defend them fails to do so, and their complaint is to no avail. More often, sympathetic listeners do not know how to reply and convey by their awkwardness or rush to reassure that the news of the assault is too much and too hard for them to bear.

Listening to the Victims of Sexual Assault

Listening to an account of sexual assault is difficult. As T. S. Eliot wrote in *Four Quartets*, "humankind/ Cannot bear very much reality." Students who have been assaulted are astute observers of what we can and cannot bear. Protective of both themselves and of us, they will tailor what they say to what we are willing to hear. It is important, therefore, to have an accurate estimate of our own capacity to listen, of the role we have or are ready to assume in a student's life and of the resources to which we can refer. Faculty members are not therapists nor are therapists parents, and the level of disclosure that is appropriate will vary according to the person, setting and circumstances. And, in fact, the cognitive processing of traumatic experience often requires repeated telling at different levels of detail and emotion, until the untoward experience becomes part of the broader narrative of the self and its experience. Our willingness to listen, therefore—whether one time in pursuit of righting a student's academic progress or repeatedly as a parent, campus minister or therapist—can help restore balance to a self upended by assault.

Achieving this balance requires the ability to exercise a reasonable degree of control over one's self and environment—the very thing that an assault denies a woman. The fact that a man gains access to a woman's body against her will, often by coercion and force, simultaneously robs her of any assurance of autonomy and renders her environment suspect and unpredictable. As one student put it, "I hate the fact that I always have to be on my toes, that I never know when I might run into him or when I might start crying, or someone might say something that sets me off. I want my life back." Reclaiming one's life therefore entails regaining the initiative in relationships and establishing an environment that is reasonably stable and predictable. Unfortunately some of the most well-meaning attempts to help can hurt in this regard.

"I am afraid to tell my family because my father and brothers will want to go out and find him and beat him up, and my mother won't want to let me out of her sight. I know they love me and mean well, but that's not what I need from them." Such sentiments are not uncommon, nor are they expressed solely in regard to family. Counselors can make sound diagnostic and therapeutic decisions that have the effect of seizing the initiative, or they can press the therapy in advance of a student's trust and confidence. Campus ministers and confessors can urge forgiveness before it is possible or invite faith in God's love when both are in doubt, and the intense relief and support gained from a student retreat can seem cruelly betrayed upon returning to the ordinary rough and tumble of campus life. Faculty members can require in class or in writing assignments personal disclosure that forces a student to reveal what she would not otherwise choose to, or they can present material in a way and at an intensity that effectively ensures that a student will feel assaulted again. Even campus groups and organizations intended to combat sexual assault can implicitly establish a single norm for recovery and participation that can preempt an individual woman's achievement or prematurely solicit her allegiance.

The goal, then, should be to listen carefully enough to follow a student's lead and, in doing so, to provide the stable and predictable environment that the restoration of trust requires. Doing this is an act of grace. But the gift may not be recognized as such by the student—one effect of a sexual assault is that it threatens the capacity to believe in a just universe, a good God and the abundance of grace. After all, a young woman would be well within her rights to ask where a just, good and gracious God was at the time of her assault.

Transformational Coping

In response to this question, the psychologist Kenneth Pargament suggests that it depends on where the student looks. In his study of how people use religion to deal with adversity, Pargament found that our first and most natural recourse is to what we have known and relied on in the past, what he calls conservational coping. Very often such recourse is successful, and the crisis is met with reserves of faith and meaning sufficient to the challenge. There are crises, however, that threaten the very foundation of faith and belief and that require a rediscovery of faith and meaning apart from what we have known, what he calls transformational coping. For college women already facing developmental challenges to what they know and believe, sexual assault can be a crisis that requires a transformation of faith.

A woman with whom I worked several years ago was raped by an acquaintance at a fraternity party. Some months after the rape, a high school friend died suddenly and unexpectedly. At the friend's funeral the priest stated in his homily that there was no explanation for what had happened, no reason for the death of someone so young and that "we simply have to go on in faith without an answer to our question, Why?" My student left the funeral disappointed and angry and resolved never to go back to church. She felt alone and was understandably shaken by the implication that if there was no explanation for her friend's death, then there was no explanation for what had happened to her. God was absent or silent in both instances.

Pargament's research suggests that while anger and fear are a natural response to the failure of religion in a time of crisis, persistently angry and negative estimations of God, the self and religious institutions are correlated with a failure to resolve the crisis and poorer mental health. He suggests that what is needed is an opportunity to think about God and the crisis in a new way, what he terms benign cognitive reframing, and to have an experience of a supportive community of faith, both of which are associated with successful coping and improved mental health. Merely exchanging one set of beliefs for another or relying on rite and ritual may give the semblance of cognitive change and of community, but they can as easily forestall the genuine transformations of mind and heart that are needed.

Fortunately this student had opportunities for both. A chance encounter with a campus minister developed into a friendship and led to a series of conversations about God and suffering that challenged many of her assumptions. And the tragic death of a fellow student prompted her to attend a memorial Mass on campus where she was surprised to find that she was not alone but part of a large congregation of young men and women hoping to find the same answers for which she had been searching. No longer wedded to angry defiance and disbelief, she was, if not yet ready to believe again, open to the possibility.

From Betrayal to Hope

In a context where minds are meant to be challenged and at a time in their lives when students are exquisitely sensitive to the shape and character of human relationships, the bridge between shaken faith and a steady grace must be built around new ways of thinking about God and a deepened experience of community. The passage from betrayal to hope, therefore, must pass through a necessary, if unbidden, transformation. And we must be willing to abide, along with students, the storms of their disbelief and the dull ache of God's seeming betrayal, their not infrequent infidelities more temporizing than deliberate and their alternating needs to hold us dear and to keep us at bay. During this time we must steadily meet each challenge with faith and confidence and thus, through our example, provide the reasons for them both. In doing so we bear witness to the grace the students are approaching and to its power to heal.

In an essay included in *Meditations From a Moveable Chair*, the late André Dubus writes about his sister's rape and its aftermath: "But one bright day her anger and hatred will turn to white ash, and she will forgive him, the rape will finally end, and the man will truly be gone, to wander in her past."

Dubus asks much of his sister and of any woman who has been raped, for forgiveness is hard and not assured and is not, in some economies of healing, necessary or desirable. But what he gets right is that healing requires change. Taken more as a prayer than a prediction, his words suggest how the betrayal of the original promise of college can be redeemed; they allow us to see that our attempts to ask and listen and believe, our willingness to be led and to bridge gaps in faith and understanding, are in their own way how the prayer is answered.

DAUGHTERS OF RAPE SPEAK OUT

Jennifer Braunschweiger

In the following selection, Jennifer Braunschweiger describes several young women who learned that they were conceived during an act of rape and the impact this knowledge has had on their lives. She reports that these women typically experienced conflicting and disturbing emotions—some fearing that they may have inherited violent tendencies from their fathers, others developing a deep distrust of men. Most, Braunschweiger writes, feel ambivalent: They are angry at their fathers for raping their mothers, yet they realize that their fathers' actions gave them life. Despite these women's understandable anger, many have a positive self-image, concluding that the circumstances of their conception have nothing to do with their own individual worth. Braunschweiger, a freelance journalist, writes frequently for *Glamour* magazine.

Julie Makimaa had been waiting for what seemed like an eternity for the couple in the adjoining hotel room to arrive. Nervous and excited, she had changed her clothes three times, finally settling on a plain black dress. She pressed her ear to the door, trying to eavesdrop, but the couples words were indistinct.

Twenty years old at the time, Makimaa had driven 11 hours from Petoskey, Michigan, to Washington, D.C., with her husband, Bob, and eight-month-old daughter, Casey, to meet the people in the next room: Julie's birth mother, Lee Ezell, and her husband, Hal. At age seven, Makimaa had learned she had been adopted. At 17, when she married, her parents had given her the records that would help her find her natural mother, and almost four years later, she located Ezell. Makimaa was moments from seeing her face for the first time, and asking an adopted child's most haunting question: Why was I given up?

At last, the doors between the rooms were opened, and Makimaa and Ezell stood staring at each other. "We have the same brown eyes, the same brown hair, the same smile," Makimaa says. After brief hugs and introductions, "My mother said, 'I want you to know the truth.'"

The fact that Makimaa was given up for adoption as an infant was only part of the story. More shocking was the event of her actual conception. Makimaa listened as Ezell recounted being invited to a pizza party at her coworker's house almost nine months to the day before Makimaa was born. When Ezell arrived at his home, however, she found herself alone with him; apparently, he had told everyone else that the party was off. "Basically, she was set up," Makimaa says. "She was sexually assaulted, escaped and ran out the door."

Ezell's rapist is Makimaa's biological father. Makimaa had been preparing herself for an unhappy tale. "But I had no idea it would be that bad," says Makimaa, now 34. "Lee was crying as she told me about the rape, and I was crying, too. I just told her, 'I'm sorry. I'm so sorry.'"

Violent Beginnings

Imagine discovering that you were conceived not in love, but in violence; learning that not only was your birth not eagerly anticipated, but also that your existence was actually forced upon your mother. Imagine finding out that you were worse than unwanted—you were a source of agony and anxiety, the flesh-and-blood reminder of a horrible violation.

Like Makimaa and countless others, a daughter who learns she was conceived in rape faces a potentially dizzying array of emotional and psychological issues. Makimaa struggled with them after she met her birth mother 14 years ago. "I've asked myself, How important to me is the fact that I was conceived in rape?" she says. "What does it really mean to me?'

Makimaa was forced to deal with feelings of abandonment associated with having been given up for adoption. But unlike other adopted kids, a daughter of rape must also wrestle with a difficult ambivalence toward her birth father, who simultaneously violated her mother and gave her life. And then there is the issue of genetics. As Makimaa succinctly puts it, "I wondered, Did I inherit some kind of evil gene? Will I risk passing it on to my children?"

Not surprisingly, experts are divided on how to answer these questions. "It would be incorrect to say that all violent behavior, including rape, is based on genes," says Alen J. Salerian, M.D., medical director of the prestigious Washington Psychiatric Center in Washington, D.C. "But in the past 10 to 15 years, genetic predisposition to certain behaviors—violence, aggression, even recklessness—has been shown to be a good possibility."

But psychologist Elizabeth Carll, Ph.D., a trauma and stress expert in Centerport, New York, agrees with Dr. Salerian only to a point. She says that even if a woman were to inherit aggressive tendencies from her rapist father, she may channel them in positive, socially acceptable ways. "She may be a great achiever in her career, or an athlete— aggression is not necessarily a bad thing," Carll says. "There's no such thing as an evil seed. There is an awful lot of rape and domestic violence in the world, so if it were true that anyone born because of them was bound to carry on that type of behavior, well, we might as well give up right now."

Untold Thousands

Other than having the circumstances of their conception in common, daughters of rape—especially those in their twenties or thirties—are difficult to identify as a group. There are no widely publicized support groups where they gather, no national statistics keeping track of them. Even if such statistics existed, they would be suspect: A woman would not necessarily know if she was pregnant for some time when she sought medical care after a rape; she might miscarry; she could choose to have an abortion. Or she might believe that the child had been fathered by her husband or boyfriend at the time. The stigma surrounding both rape and single motherhood—particularly 25 to 35 years ago, when Makimaa's mother was raped—might discourage her from reporting what happened at all.

Although it's impossible to get a precise count of all the children conceived in rape, it's safe to say that the number is sizable. The National Violence Against Women survey sponsored by the National Institute of Justice and the Centers for Disease Control and Prevention, released in 1998, estimated that more than 876,000 rapes occur each year in the United States. There's no practical way to determine the exact number of children born of these rapes. But a study published in 1996 by the Medical University of South Carolina in Charleston estimated that 32,101 pregnancies result from rape each year in the United States. The study—based on three years of research involving more than 4,000 women—also found that 38 percent of the pregnancies were carried to term, with 32 percent of the children kept by their mothers and 6 percent given up for adoption. According to this study, then, more than 12,000 children are born as a result of rape each year in the United States.

They include Pam Stenzel, 34, from Heron Lake, Minnesota, the founder of a national teen-abstinence advocacy group called Straight Talk. Adopted as an infant, Stenzel was 13 when she found out from a woman at her adoption agency that her mother had been raped by a stranger and become pregnant with Stenzel at age 15. Dina Atchison (a pseudonym; all names are real except where indicated), 30, a teacher's assistant in Los Angeles, was told by her mother eight years ago that Atchison's rapist father was the pastor at the parish house where her mother once lived. Atchison was raised by her mother and says they have always been "extremely close—especially since I found out she was raped." Mary Hunt, 33, of Ocean Township, New Jersey, used information from her adoption records to track down her birth mother 10 years ago. Much to her shock, Hunt found out that she had been conceived during an acquaintance rape. "My birth mom was afraid to scream or yell, because she had three small children in the apartment," says Hunt, who now works for a commuter-ferry company.

One prominent personality who revealed that she was conceived in rape is Faith Daniels, the host of her own NBC talk show from 1991 to 1993. In 1993, during the taping of a show about women who get pregnant as a result of rape, Daniels said that she herself had been conceived in this way. Like most of the women interviewed for this article, Daniels was certainly disturbed to learn that her mother was raped, but still sees her own life in a positive light. "It really doesn't matter how you were conceived, only what you've become," Daniels said, praising her adoptive parents for raising her in a loving home.

Hunt echoes Daniels' sentiments. "I may have come from a terrible event, but I'm not a bad person," says Hunt, who, in addition to her work for the ferry company, runs a nonprofit agency that helps terminally ill adoptees find their families. "To me, the man who fathered me is nothing. It's not like I feel there's a hole in my life. I was raised by wonderful parents, and I have a positive impact on the world around me, so I don't think my conception was an accident."

All but one of the women interviewed for this story were conceived before abortion was safe and legal in this country. Many hospitals now routinely offer rape victims medical care that includes emergency contraception. So it stands to reason that, regardless of how high the number of children born of rape is today, it was most likely even higher in the 1960s, when the crime was regarded differently than it is now. "Back then, there were no rape crisis centers, and there was no language to describe rape perpetrated by your husband or someone you knew," says Mary P. Koss, Ph.D., professor of public health at the University of Arizona in Tucson and an expert on rape. "Also, abortion was illegal and thus accessible only to the very wealthy; they could travel out of the country to have the procedure performed. Most rape survivors simply covered up the rape."

Women who did report rapes to the authorities in the 1960s were often met with disbelief or even hostility and blamed for having somehow provoked the attack. Until the 1970s, when the feminist movement demanded legal reforms, rape laws placed an unfair burden on the victim. They required corroborating evidence from witnesses and evidence of physical resistance from the woman; they also allowed the woman's prior sexual history to be admitted into evidence in rape trials. Raped in the 1960s or early 1970s, the mothers of the women interviewed for this story had no safe, legal choice. Alone and pregnant, they carried their babies to term, and in many cases, gave them up for adoption.

Tracy Wright (a pseudonym) is 35 years old and a lobbyist for higher education in Washington, D.C. She remembers clearly the night 18 years ago when she found out that she had been conceived in rape. Then a sophomore in high school, Wright was in the living room talking with her mother, Clara, and started asking about her birth father, Clara's first husband: How had he and her mother met? What was his personality like? Clara calmly told Wright that they'd met when she was 16 and had gotten married when she was just a junior in high school. They had their first child, Wright's older sister, when Clara was 19, and the baby put a strain on what was already a troubled marriage. Clara's husband expected to be waited on hand and foot and always to get his way, Wright says, adding, "As she was telling me all about him, she said out of the blue, 'But you weren't planned.'"

"What do you mean by that?" Wright asked.

"Well," Clara responded, "we were having a fight—"

Wright pauses, then continues, "My mom said, 'We were having a fight. And I ran out of the house. And he ran after me.' He raped her outside in the yard. She took my sister and packed her bags and left."

"I was dumbfounded," Wright says. "On the one hand, I felt badly for her. But I also thought, Why did you have to tell me that?"

Psychologists agree that a child who finds out she was conceived in rape will often have a hard time handling the information. Dr. Salerian says he admitted a woman to his facility in April 1999 because she had become suicidal after discovering that her father, whom she had never met, had raped her mother. "It was all the more traumatic because her mother also told her that she had contemplated an abortion," Dr. Salerian says. "This information was very hurtful and intensified my patient's depression."

Wright says the news about her conception hit her hard. She was angry at her mother for "unburdening herself of this mantle that she'd carried. I was like, 'I feel like s— now. I don't even feel wanted.'"

Wright does remember meeting her father as a child. After the divorce, he insisted on visitation rights—with Wright's older sister. He was allowed on the condition that he see Wright, too. Only four years old, Wright recalls her father favoring her sister. "He didn't want me there; it was evident. I was being treated differently than my sister, but I didn't know why," she says. Wright hasn't seen her father since then but remains curious: "Who is he? What does he do for a living?"

Ambivalent Feelings About Rapist Fathers

All of the women interviewed for this story share a strong curiosity about their fathers. Some, understandably, feel angry not just toward him, but toward all men. "I have a hard time trusting or believing what any man says," confesses Atchison. In early 1968, Atchison's mother moved into the parish house of a Los Angeles church. Twenty-five years old and an unmarried mom at the time, Atchison's mother was fleeing an abusive relationship with a live-in boyfriend. The pastor, a family friend, let her live there while she got back on her feet. But one night that May, the pastor entered the house while her son was asleep. "She was petite. He was a big guy," Atchison says, her voice thick with emotion. "She did her best to fight him off, but she couldn't."

The pastor kicked Atchison's mother out of the house when he found out she was pregnant, but she never reported the rape. "She didn't think anyone would take her word over the word of a so-called respected minister," she says ruefully.

Atchison was born January 21, 1969. Her mother got married two years after the rape, and Atchison grew up believing that her mother's husband was her father. But one day in December 1991, Atchison's mother tearfully revealed the truth. "She said I was the child of her rape," Atchison recalls. "We were crying, holding one another, trying to console one another." Two weeks later, Atchison went to see her birth father preach. She sat toward the back of the church and fixed her eyes on him. "He didn't know I was there. His sermon was about forgiving those who have done you wrong. I was so angry. I felt he was hiding behind a robe, up in his pulpit, preaching the word of God, but having been guilty of vicious acts."

Today, the minister is still preaching, and Atchison is still angry. "I have a problem with men. I don't think I'll ever be able to be married."

But Atchison's reaction seems to be the exception rather than the rule. Most of the women interviewed say they feel more or less ambivalent about their rapist fathers. "*I* wasn't raped," says Stenzel. "I'm angry at all men who would abuse women in that way. But specifically toward him? I can't feel that."

Dr. Salerian says that Stenzel's feelings are understandable and, indeed, not uncommon. "If a woman has gone through her own pain and moved on, there's absolutely nothing wrong with that from a psychological perspective," Dr. Salerian continues. "Life itself is the greatest cure for experiences like this. There's nothing that says these women ought to be obsessed or preoccupied with the trauma of their origin."

By the same token, it's not surprising that "the trauma of their origin" influences the lives of many daughters of rape in a profound way, shaping everything from their political and religious beliefs to the careers or volunteer work they pursue. Many of the women interviewed for this story are devoutly religious and strongly anti-abortion. For instance, Rebecca Wasser-Kiessling, 30, from Rochester Hills, Michigan, is a family law attorney with a specialty in what she calls "procreational rights." Her mother was raped by a stranger at knifepoint and, while pregnant with Wasser-Kiessling, was thwarted twice (once by a major ice storm) in her attempts to get an abortion—which Wasser-Kiessling sees as the intervening hand of God. Today, she is a member of Right to Life of Michigan and on the advisory board of Michigan Nurses for Life.

Soon after Wasser-Kiessling was born, her mother put her up for adoption. The two were reunited in 1988 and are close today. Their relationship hasn't always been quite so rosy, however. For the first several years that they knew each other, Wasser-Kiessling says, her mother maintained that she had wanted an abortion after the rape. "I had already forgiven her about that, but about five years ago, she said she was, in fact, glad that she didn't abort me," Wasser-Kiessling says. "Now I see it as my mission to help women and unborn children through my law practice."

Not all rape daughters learn to cope so well. Wright says she and her mother remain close, but have never again been able to discuss the rape. "It was a double whammy of rejection knowing that my father didn't want me, then learning about the circumstances of my conception.

"I have nothing but admiration for my mom," Wright continues, "for what she went through and the sacrifices she's made in her life so that my sister and I could have a good life." But, she admits, she wishes her mother hadn't told her about the rape. "We haven't talked about it since she first told me, and I've never really understood her motivation for telling me. I can only surmise that I was her confidante. She relied on me quite heavily—I was her daughter but also her friend. But I think there are some things a parent shouldn't tell her child. Why did she have to unburden herself to me?"

Raped and Left for Dead

Women who were conceived as a result of a rape by a stranger are confronted by a unique—and perhaps more intense—set of emotional issues. Cathi Pickavet is 25 years old and an associate editor at a computer magazine in Sacramento, California. Her mother, who was 21 and a virgin at the time she was raped, was attacked in the parking lot of a Montgomery Ward department store in Panorama City, California, on October 17, 1972, while out for a walk. The rapist stabbed her and left her for dead (he was never caught). But after lying for nearly an hour alone in the dark, Pickavet's mother struggled back to her apartment.

"I'm a product of this heinous act, and if I get lost in thinking about it, it can be very disturbing," Pickavet says. "He didn't just rape her, he brutalized her. I'm half this person who stabbed my mother four times and nearly killed her. What does that make me?"

When she was young, Pickavet's natural curiosity about where she came from was heightened by the fact that she didn't have a father. One day when she was seven, a friend of her mother's told Pickavet about the rape. "I had been asking questions—'Who's my father?'—so she told me. I couldn't understand exactly what rape was, of course, and she didn't explain, but I remember being satisfied by the answer. I stopped asking questions," Pickavet says.

In fact, she stopped asking for 16 years. "It simply was not something that my mom and I discussed. I was more concerned about the question of my sexuality," says Pickavet, who is a lesbian. She says she felt even before she was a teenager that she was gay, and that it caused no small amount of conflict in her life. "In high school, I was very outgoing. I was into sports, and everyone knew me. But I'd go home and sit alone in my room and be miserable. I tried twice to commit suicide."

In college, she came out, "and then I moved on to dealing with the fact that I was conceived in rape." Pickavet still struggles to find words to describe how she feels about the circumstances of her creation. She's angry, but at whom? "I can't really be mad at my father— he's just a concept," she says. "What I feel is mainly frustration."

Upon finding out, at age 18, that she was conceived when her mother was attacked by a suspected serial rapist, Wasser-Kiessling felt "ugly and unwanted. I wondered, Who would ever love me? Who would want to marry me, procreate with me, since I had criminal genes?" Wasser-Kiessling says she entered one bad relationship after another, including one with a man who beat her. "To try to feel better about myself—to medicate the pain of knowing how I was conceived— I would jump into relationships," she says.

Ultimately, she says, no relationship with a man could help her rebuild her self-esteem, so she turned to God. "I believe that God rewarded my birth mother for the suffering she endured, and that I am a gift to her. The serial rapist is not my creator; God is."

Pickavet is still overwhelmed when she considers how she came into being. She is close to her mother but refers to herself as a "half-rapist" and to her father as "my sperm donor." Above all, she is conflicted by her mixed ethnicity. All of the family Pickavet knows—her mother, grandmother, aunts and uncles (who, she says, have always been very loving toward her)—are white, but to the stranger on the street she looks black. "I grew up in white society, and all my relatives are white," she explains. "But when people look at me, they don't see a white person."

In 1997, when Pickavet at last discussed her conception with her mother, she asked her how she felt when she found out she was pregnant. "She said she was overjoyed," Pickavet remembers, adding that her mom is a devout Catholic. "I said, 'You were honestly happy? You never had the feeling like, God, what is this thing inside me? I don't want it!' But she said, 'Never.'"

Parting with the Past

Makimaa, who nervously met her birth mother, Lee Ezell, 14 years ago, now works for the nonprofit Family Resource Council in Holland, Michigan. She notes that time has been a great healer of the wounds she initially felt upon finding out she was conceived in rape. "The first two or three months were very difficult," she says. "I felt a lot of pain and confusion. But I have stability in my life—a loving husband, and now two children. My life isn't necessarily defined by that one event. Influenced by it, yes, but not defined by it."

Cheerful and friendly, Makimaa jokes about her poor husband having to contend with two mothers-in-law. But her relationship with

Ezell is special to her whole family, especially her daughter, Casey, now 15, and her son, Herb, 13, who are both close to their "extra" grandmother. Makimaa and Ezell speak at least once a month about their lives, their families, their children.

Makimaa now knows her birth father's name, but since her mother left her job so soon after she was raped, she does not know if he's aware he has a child. "In the beginning," Makimaa says, "I was very angry at him for having hurt Lee." If Makimaa were to search for him today, she says, it would be for the purpose of asking him just one thing: "Do you realize the pain that you caused my birth mother? I want him to ask forgiveness for that."

It is a stunning fact of these stories that in each case, the mother was able to overcome her loathing for her rapist and instead find joy in her love for her child. "While awful things do happen to us, sometimes wonderful things come out of it," says Carll. "A wonderful daughter would certainly be something positive that might help to erase some of the negative memories of a rape."

Nonetheless, before her mother reassured her, Makimaa worried that she would always be a bad reminder of the rape. And Ezell did at first struggle with memories. "But she made up her mind that I would not be a negative thing in her life," remembers Makimaa. "She does not see me as part of him at all, but as part of her, and as someone else who was innocent, like she was."

Makimaa turned 21 that weekend in Washington, D.C., in 1985, and they all celebrated together: Ezell and her husband, and Makimaa and her husband, and Casey, Ezell's first grandchild. The celebratory cake bore just one candle, Makimaa says, "because it was my mom's first birthday with me."

Today, Makimaa has found peace with the questions that troubled her when she first learned of her mother's rape. "If anything, finding out only solidified for me more the value of each of our lives. It doesn't matter if you are not a planned child conceived in an act of love. What's important is who you are as a person and what you do with your life. The circumstances of your conception can't determine that."

CHAPTER 4

PERSONAL PERSPECTIVES ON RAPE

I WAS RAPED

Stephanie Booth

Stephanie Booth was raped during the summer before her senior year in high school. In the following account, originally written for *Teen* magazine, she describes how she was violently attacked by a man who sneaked up behind her as she was walking home alone after a party. Booth writes that she immediately filed a police report and underwent examinations by medical person-nel, but she was never able to identify her rapist and therefore could not bring criminal charges against him. She admits that she initially blamed herself for the attack, but crisis counselors and a therapist helped her work through her emotional turmoil during the weeks following the rape.

I thought the summer before my senior year in high school would be the best summer of my life. Besides landing an awesome job at a hotel in Santa Fe, New Mexico, I'd gotten back with Drew, my boyfriend off and on for two years.

Drew and I had always had a rocky relationship. He was so sweet and fun to be around, but he was also a total flirt. I hoped this time things would be different.

That first weekend we were officially back together, Drew asked me to go to a party with him. I knew there would be lots of other girls there, which is probably why I bought a sexy sundress to wear. I did-n't want Drew to take his eyes off me.

"You look great," he said when he picked me up. But as soon as we got to the party, he was in flirt mode again, hugging everyone and introducing himself to cute girls. I didn't know anyone else there, so I hung out in the backyard talking to this guy named Marco who Drew introduced me to.

Marco couldn't stop talking about himself, telling me what a hot-shot quarterback he was and how much his new Jeep cost. I was hoping Drew would come rescue me as Marco rambled on, tossing back beer after beer. But finally I was so mad that I started to walk home alone.

I Thought I Was Safe

It was almost midnight, but I never thought twice about walking at night, even in downtown Santa Fe; I knew the area like the back of

Reprinted from Stephanie Booth, "I Was Raped," *Teen*, October 1998. Reprinted with permission from *Teen*.

my hand. I was behind the old Woolworth when I heard footsteps. Before I could turn around, I felt hands grabbing my hips.

"Shhh," someone whispered into my ear.

For a second I felt really relieved—maybe Drew wasn't such a jerk after all. But the next thing I knew, I was on my back in the middle of the alley. Someone was on top of me, pinning me down by the shoulders, jamming his knee between my legs. I couldn't see his face clearly in the dark, but he had on a white button-down shirt with the sleeves rolled up—that's the thing I saw and remembered the most.

I kicked and screamed and clawed at him, but he was so heavy on top of me that I couldn't move.

"Shhh," he kept telling me. "Shhh."

I kept screaming anyway, but no one heard me. He lifted my dress and pulled down my underwear. Then I heard him unbuckle his belt.

I don't know how long it was before he climbed off me. It felt like hours. He stood up and said, "Not bad." When I heard his voice, I thought, It's Marco.

Screaming for Help

I dragged myself up and stumbled into the street. Every part of me ached, and I was bleeding. Then I started screaming again as though I'd never stop.

The manager of a hotel heard me and helped me inside. A police officer came and drove me to the emergency room. I was crying and shaking, saying, "I'm so sorry!" to everyone. I was sure all of this was my fault: I shouldn't have worn that dress. I shouldn't have been walking alone.

"You should be able to walk down the street at any time and be safe," the rape crisis counselor at the hospital said. "No one deserves what you've been through."

Then why did I feel like such a slut? I'd never felt more humiliated in my life.

When my parents arrived, I couldn't look my dad in the eye. Drew showed up, too, and he was crying harder than I was, which made me feel even worse.

I was in the emergency room for hours. They did a "rape kit," sticking cotton swabs under my fingernails and pulling hair out of my head and my pubic area for evidence. My ripped, bloody clothes were put in a plastic bag for the police.

After the doctor examined me, I filled out a police report. My parents had gone to get the car, and Drew put his arm around me while I wrote down what had happened. But when I mentioned Marco, he told me to stop and take a deep breath: Wasn't it possible that I was really freaked out and looking for someone to blame?

I didn't know what or who to believe.

"It's over with," Drew said. "You're going to be OK. That's the important thing. Just don't think about it."

I didn't trust myself enough to press charges, so I let it go.

Emotional Trauma

For weeks afterward, I was so depressed. I couldn't go to work, and I didn't want to talk to my friends. Every guy, whether I knew him or not, seemed like a threat. Even though it was summer, I hid beneath baggy jeans and sweatshirts.

The physical part of the rape was horrible, but the emotional agony was worse. Each time I had a nightmare about it, I woke up soaked in sweat. And I was so mad at myself—why couldn't I remember what happened?

Drew called me every day, even after I told him I just wanted to be friends. He gave me a shoulder to cry on and reminded me that this wasn't the end of the world. My parents were patient with me, too, but I could tell they didn't know what to say. My dad bought me a can of pepper spray so I'd feel safer, but it made me feel like he thought I should have been more careful.

I talked the most to people at the crisis hotlines. I also saw a therapist, and it helped to hear someone say, "You'll get stronger. You won't feel like this forever." It was hard to believe.

A few weeks after it happened, the police called me down to the station to look through mug shots. I flipped through them, hoping I'd say, "There he is! That's him!"

Sometimes I felt so positive that it was Marco who raped me. But if I knew it was him, I would have told the police everything that night. I would have done everything I could to stop him from doing it again. But all I could really remember was a man forcing himself on me. For a long time, I thought I'd be "cured" if I knew for sure. At the same time, I just wanted to forget it ever happened.

Now, finally, I realize it's important to remember that my rape happened, even if I can't identify the rapist. Being raped was a horrifying experience, but in a weird way it opened my eyes to a lot of things: Like how really sacred your body is. And how total strangers can come out of nowhere and help you through an ordeal. And how you're probably tougher than you ever imagined.

It's true. I'm living proof.

Rape Was Just the Beginning of My Ordeal

Marjorie Preston

In the following selection, journalist Marjorie Preston discusses her long road to recovery after being raped. Preston was brutally attacked by a stranger who broke into her home in the middle of the night. During the first few months after the rape, Preston writes, she thought she was handling everything quite well, but she was actually in shock and detached from her emotions. Eventually she began drinking, overeating, and using tranquilizers in an attempt to suppress her anxiety and depression. The lengthy legal process only intensified her emotional trauma, she maintains. A few years after the crime, Preston finally found a friend who was willing to let her talk about the rape and its aftermath. According to Preston, this friendship enabled her to begin to rebuild her life and recover from her ordeal.

I kissed my five-year-old daughter and waved good-bye as she walked toward the airport terminal, hand-in-hand with her father. They were off to Florida on vacation, and I looked forward to a few days alone. As a second-year college student, I planned to catch up on homework while Joanie [not her real name] was away.

I had returned to college as a thirty-three-year-old single mom, fulfilling a longtime dream to study communications. Life was so busy in 1991 that when the local news reported that a prisoner being transported from court in my town had escaped from custody, I hardly blinked—the fugitive was a petty thief, and Media, Pennsylvania, was so quaint and quiet that I referred to it as Mayberry.

Joanie and I lived on the first floor of a grand old Victorian house, complete with high ceilings and a slate fireplace. For all its charm, security was rather lax, but that was the furthest thing from my mind that night. I worked until two A.M., then tumbled into bed.

The Attack

A couple of hours later, I thought I was having a nightmare. I couldn't breathe, and began to thrash around struggling to wake. Then, I felt gloved hands pressing hard on my eyes and mouth. A stranger stood over me in the dark, and I heard a man's soft voice at my ear. "Where's the money?" Though his hands covered my mouth, inside I was already screaming. *Oh, no. Not this.* I had no money, but I told him he could take my car. "I don't want your car," he said. "Turn over."

That's when I panicked. "I can't," I said. "I'm too afraid. Please don't make me." But he was merciless. In the same soft voice, the stranger ordered me to do as he said, warning that if I saw his face, he would kill me. "I have a knife," he said.

Now I know how I'm going to die, I thought. *Tonight I'm going to be murdered in my bed.* I wondered who would find me. *And, oh God, who will tell my child?*

My attacker twisted my face into the mattress, and instinctively, I started talking about my little girl. "She's on vacation. She's coming home in a few days. I need to be here for her. She's only five." *Maybe he won't kill me if I can make him know me.*

"I won't hurt you," he said, as he started to rape me. Face down on the bed, I strained to catch a glimpse of him from the corner of my eye. *Remember everything,* I told myself. *If I live, I will be able to tell.*

Perhaps forty minutes later—though I will never be sure—he seemed to be finishing. Under my breath, I whispered my prayers, hoping the knife wouldn't hurt. But he climbed off and was gone, soundless as a ghost. When I raised my head, I was alone; my lace curtains billowed around an open window. I slammed the window shut and ran through the apartment, screaming. I had never been so frightened—or so angry—in my life

I immediately called my parents, but there was no answer, so I dialed the police. Within minutes, half a dozen squad cars pulled into the driveway. Briefly, I told them what had happened, and they drove me to the hospital. I cried just once, remembering that my five-year-old often crept into the bed where I had just been raped. *Thank God she wasn't home,* I thought.

Delaware County Women Against Rape sent a volunteer to the emergency room, who warned that I could experience a range of emotions, from shock and denial to anger and depression. I waved her away. "I'm fine," I said wearily. "I just want to go home."

The next morning, I was driven from the hospital to the police station, where I wrote out a statement. I finally reached my mother, who arrived minutes after my call. "Mom, I thought he was going to cut my throat," I said. I hadn't seen my mother cry in years, but she cried then. By the time she drove me home, my father had already installed bars on my bedroom window.

At first, friends and family overwhelmed me with offers of help, but I refused them all. I felt oddly euphoric; I was alive, and impressed at how well I was handling this.

In reality, my emotions stopped functioning the night I was raped.

Shock enabled me to think, and kept me from becoming hysterical. It may have saved my life. But that sense of disassociation lingered, keeping me totally out of touch with my feelings. In fact, when newspapers carried stories about the "brutal rape," I felt as if I were reading about someone else.

One week after the rape, Jeffrey Andrew Page, the escaped burglar, was captured in a Philadelphia hotel room. He was a primary suspect in my case, but the investigation was not complete for several months, until DNA test results were in.

Six months later, at the preliminary hearing, I sat perfectly composed, ready to testify. I was convinced that the trauma was behind me. But that day I started to unravel. As Page entered the courtroom, I began to shake. On the stand, I found myself crying uncontrollably as I described the night I was raped.

Substance Abuse and Overeating

For months afterward, sleep was difficult. I would bolt out of bed in the middle of the night, heart racing, certain someone was in the room with me. Tranquilizers kept the anxiety at bay; so did food. I would do anything to divert my racing thoughts. Soon I added alcohol to the mix to help me sleep. Between overeating and drinking too much, I gained sixty-seven pounds in less than a year. It was strange to look in the mirror and see myself so puffy, so haggard. I now realize I had made myself as unattractive as possible to stave off any man's attention. If I was ugly, I would be safe.

Now I ached to talk about the crime, but family and friends were reluctant listeners. For one thing, they had dealt with their reactions months earlier, and had moved on. Furthermore, the details of this crime were so intimate. It's often said that rape is not about sex, but violence. That's not true. Rape may be about violence and domination for the predator, but it is also absolutely about sex. A man I did not know forced me into an act of intercourse. Sometimes I thought if he had beaten me, even tried to kill me, it would have been more acceptable. But this was sexual, and people found it embarrassing.

After two years of suppressing my fears, I eventually acknowledged that my life was heading in the wrong direction. Though I managed to keep my drinking inconspicuous—I was going to school, and working at the college radio station part-time—I still used alcohol and tranquilizers to cope. I hoped that a thirty-day substance abuse program would help.

Hatred and Depression

Arriving at the treatment center, I discussed my problem with an intake worker: I had been raped, I said. Perhaps understandably, I had a fierce mistrust of men. Drinking had become my refuge. He agreed that inpatient treatment would be a good choice for me. But after I checked in, I realized that every other patient at the center was a man, and learned that many of them had just been released from prison. When I protested, a therapist encouraged me to "bond" with them. I fled the center the next day.

Not only did I feel hatred for the first time in my life, but I was also emotionally distant from my daughter during that time. The depression that followed the attack made me less of a mom to Joanie. She was five at the time, eight when the trial was over. Now she's a teenager, and sometimes I still yearn for the countless priceless moments of little girlhood that I didn't share fully with her.

When Joanie was little, I told her, "Someone hurt Mommy. That's why I'm so sad." Eventually, when she was older, I told her what happened. But she has never been able to understand why I was not truly there for her all those years. Deep down, I believe she thinks I let her down. Deep down, I agree.

I never saw the face of my attacker, so the case against Jeffrey Page turned on physical evidence. After waiting months for the results, a DNA match of semen ultimately implicated him, leading to charges of rape, simple assault, robbery, terroristic threats and unlawful restraint, as well as burglary and possession of an instrument of crime

I thought the case would move along smoothly from that point, but because DNA cases were relatively new—mine was one of the first in Pennsylvania—the defense protested using such testing, and a trial date was postponed for a year. Two more years of legal wrangling would follow.

Almost three years had passed, and the trial was still pending. Depressed and anxious, I had quit school and settled for a clerical job in real estate. Once an ambitious, purposeful woman, I was just marking time. I felt so isolated, and no longer talked about the rape. Lucky for me, a friend had given me a squat, sad-faced Boston terrier; that little dog became my confidant.

The Beginning of Recovery

Then, one day in January 1994, I found another. I was at the real-estate office when I was notified of yet another trial delay. Frustrated, I broke down, right in front of my boss, Donna Keegan. Everything spilled out, and I regretted it instantly. It was unprofessional. I scarcely knew Donna. For a moment, she was subdued. Then she said, "You must have been so scared."

I remember how surprised I was when she asked me to tell her what happened, and how desperately I needed to share it. Hesitantly, I started talking, and she never stopped me. I described the crime and the aftermath, the alcohol and the depression, and the insensitivity of the legal system. For months, Donna let me tell my story again and again—until it no longer ruled me, and memories of the rape no longer erupted in my dreams.

Gradually, as I released the poisonous feelings inside, the behaviors I had used to stifle my emotions were no longer necessary. It took time and patience and a few false starts, but ultimately, I stopped relying on food, drink and drugs to calm me. The weight—my shield of armor—fell away. It was the beginning of my recovery.

The trial was finally rescheduled for March 21, 1994. As the prosecutor questioned me, I looked at him pleadingly, hoping, to no avail, he would skip the more intimate questions. During the cross-examination by Page's attorneys, I was forced to look in the defendant's direction, but Page never looked at me, never said a word and never took the stand. Finally, on March 25, Jeffrey Page was found guilty, and a month later, he was sentenced to nearly fifteen and a half to thirty-three years in prison. I had been avenged.

Strange as it sounds, I wouldn't trade my experience for anyone else's life. It is a measure of me, of what I am capable of enduring, and I'm proud of the life I've rebuilt. In the years since the rape, I've successfully pursued a career in journalism. When I started covering the crime beat, I was gratified that victims found it easy to talk to me.

Just recently, I interviewed a woman who had been kidnapped and repeatedly assaulted. She was numb, just as I had been. During our conversation, she wondered aloud if she would ever recover. I told her, "You'll get there. But remember, this process has a beginning, a middle and an end—unfortunately, the middle is the longest part." She will never be the same, but with love and support, she can recover. I know. Once I was raped, too. But it was a long time ago.

FACING DOWN MY RAPIST

Alice Sebold

At age eighteen, Alice Sebold was violently raped while walking back to her dorm on a college campus after a party. In the following selection, she describes the difficult process that led to her rapist's conviction and imprisonment. In some ways, Sebold explains, her decision to prosecute her rapist was relatively easy because he was not a friend or relative but a stranger who left her bloodied and bruised. However, Sebold still had to face the indignities of an investigation and courtroom trial that required her to discuss her traumatic rape in public; moreover, participating in a rape conviction left her vulnerable to the possibility that her attacker would seek revenge after being released from prison. In the end, though, Sebold believes that she made the right choice by facing her fears and winning justice. Sebold is the author of *Lucky*, a memoir about her rape and recovery.

There is a moment I hold onto from the day I took the witness stand to give my testimony at the trial of my rapist. The moment had nothing to do with the questions I was asked. It was the moment I met my attacker's eyes. It was brief, and others might see it as a small triumph, but to me it was enormous: My eyes did not waver and eventually he looked away.

I had been warned, by the assistant district attorneys handling my case and by the detective who escorted me during the trial, that the one thing I must avoid in the courtroom was looking directly at my rapist. It made sense. The A.D.A. wanted me to stay focused on his questions, and seeing my rapist, really looking at him, might throw me off.

But I knew instinctively that *not* looking at him would only confirm his power over me, the power he wrested from me when he attacked me one year earlier. I was 18, a college freshman and a virgin on that late spring night when I walked through a park on the way back to campus from a party. The rapist grabbed me from behind and dragged me into a tunnel scattered with broken glass where, for two hours, he raped and sodomized me.

Identifying My Rapist

Unlike many rape victims, I reported the rape to the police immediately. They couldn't find him—and, although I saw his face clearly that night, I couldn't find his photo in any of their mug shot books. Against all advice and predictions, I returned to school the following fall. It was there, six months after my rapist let me go with a promise to kill me if I reported him, that I ran into him on a street near campus in broad daylight. His confidence in my fear then was so strong that he actually greeted me. "Hey, girl," he said. "Don't I know you from somewhere?" I did know him, but I was too frightened at that moment to point out my rapist to the policeman who was standing nearby. Later that day at the police station, though, the cop was able to help me identify the man who passed me on the street. He was arrested 10 days later and the yearlong process of hearings, lineups and courtroom appearances began.

There was no way to know whether or not I would win my case. The evidence was strong—the semen collected in my rape kit was consistent with that of the man on trial, but there was no conclusive DNA evidence: At the time of my trial, DNA evidence wasn't yet being used. I was able to positively identify my rapist—an ex-con with a record—but there was no corroborating witness. My rapist was black; I am white. His attorney would argue that I could not distinguish one black man from another. And, even if I could, wasn't it more than likely that I had lost my virginity consensually earlier that night and merely chose to blame it on a black man I met in the park?

While the A.D.A. was asking me to describe my rapist I looked up and over at the defense table. I had not glanced his way when entering the court. Now I did. The rest of the courtroom fell away the moment I met his eyes. It was just the two of us all over again. I was accusing; he was denying. I continued answering the questions put to me by the A.D.A., but at that moment I was engaged in another power struggle with my rapist. This time, I was letting him know not only that he had not destroyed me but also that I intended to destroy him: To put him, for as long as I could, behind bars. I looked him in the eye; he looked back, then looked away.

How Many Rapists Are Convicted?

The estimated number of attempted or completed rapes and sexual assaults declined from 485,000 in 1993 to 333,000 in 1998, according to the U.S. Department of Justice National Crime Victimization Survey. But the proportion of women who report their rapes and sexual assaults to law enforcement continues to hover around 31 percent. The most common reasons given by women for not reporting these crimes are the belief that it is a private and personal matter and they fear reprisal from the assailant, according to reports from the Rape Abuse and Incest National Network (RAINN). For the 68 percent of rape victims who already know their assailants (according to a U.S. Department of Justice 1994–1995 survey), fear of reprisal makes sense.

Sadly, a report by Bureau of Justice statistician Lawrence A. Greenfeld indicates that only half of reported rapes from 1990 to 1995 led to arrests; half to two thirds of arrests led to convictions; and about two thirds of convicted rapists ended up serving prison time, while others were granted probation, or penalized with community service hours and fines. Quick work with a calculator indicates that only an estimated 5 to 7 percent of all rapists (including unreported rapes) are sent to jail. "Although the rape laws have improved dramatically over the past 25 years, it's still far from a perfect system," notes RAINN Executive Director Debbie Andrews. Organizations like RAINN, which provide free rape hot lines and focus on victim support and advocacy, can help victims comprehend the rewards of reporting and pursuing their attackers. DNA evidence is putting more rapists behind bars every year, but the chances of a conviction drop to zero when a rape goes unreported.

My Triumph over the Rape

In comparison to many victims, my decision to face my rapist was an easy one. He was not my father or friend or lover, and my rape would have been hard to hide. I returned to my dorm bloody and bruised, with glass and leaves caked to my hair and clothes. I was taken to the hospital in a screaming ambulance. The police interviewed me during the vaginal examination, and later, I went to the station and did the work required to initiate a case—filing an affidavit, reviewing mug shot books. It committed me to nothing, but it left the door open for the triumph that I felt not at the end of the trial—when my rapist was remanded to jail and shackles were placed on his wrists and feet—but in the midst of the trial, when his defense ploys still could have worked, when the A.D.A. prosecuting my case still could have faltered. By suffering the indignities of that night, I staked my claim for a later opportunity to put my rapist behind bars.

In defiance of the grim statistics about rape convictions, my rapist was arrested, convicted and sent to prison. He received the maximum sentence possible on six of the seven counts with which he was charged: 8⅓ to 25 years. But if I had to pinpoint the moment when my triumph over the rape began, I would say it was when I met his eyes. And I could never have gotten to that moment without pointing a finger, without saying, as free of shame as I could manage, that I had been raped and that I wanted to report it.

My rapist was released from prison early in 1999 after serving a 17-year term. He is classified by his state criminal justice system as the most violent type of offender. If I let my mind wander down a dark path, I can make myself very frightened about the possibility of his seeking some violent revenge. But I have too many things to look forward to. What I have come to believe is that the pursuit of justice is a leap of faith: To believe in it, you must walk in the face of your fear every day. When I chose to report the rape, I chose to stand vulnerable to my rapist's revenge and society's misconceptions of what it meant to be a victim of rape. There is still no question at all in my mind: I made the right choice.

WHY I REFUSE TO GIVE UP JOGGING AFTER DARK

Andrea Todd

In the following selection, New York resident and freelance writer Andrea Todd discusses her preference for jogging in the evening despite the warnings she has received from friends and family members who fear for her safety. Although Todd recognizes the possibility of being assaulted or raped, she states that she refuses to live like a victim by giving up running at the times of her choice. Antifemale violence is everywhere, Todd surmises, but women should not let the potential for violence keep them from living the kind of life they choose.

I moved to New York from California several years ago "to be a writer," and have been almost impossible to reach ever since. Like lots of freelancers, I shuttle from sublet to sublet or stay with friends; I'm often between jobs and unable to pay my phone bill every month. It's not unusual for my mother to punch in my phone number only to hear that it has been temporarily disconnected.

The only way she can reach me at all is wherever I happen to be working at that moment—and the first question she's likely to ask whomever picks up the phone is: "Have *you* seen her? She's *alive*, right?" If I'm not available, she'll leave a message, something like, if she doesn't hear from me in 48 hours she'll start planning my memorial service.

An Eerie Omen?

A couple of months ago I received just such a message from Mom after a friend of mine in New York had called her, wanting to know where I was. "They found a body," my mother explained. "Someone thinks it's Andrea."

I must admit that when I read about the body that had been dumped into a tractor-trailer in the West Village, I couldn't help noting the similarities. "Check it out," I remarked to a friend. "Five-five, 105 pounds, between 23 and 28 years old, reddish brown hair, out running down where I used to run." The police sketch looked a little

Reprinted from Andrea Todd, "Running Late," *The New York Times*, November 6, 1994. Reprinted with permission from the author.

like me, too. Same broad cheekbones, same pointed chin and narrow forehead, same thickish hair.

Another friend who saw the sketch thought it looked enough like me that she took some snapshots down to the police. The detective studied the pictures, then asked casually when she had seen or spoken to me last.

"I thought for sure it was you," she told me later that week, after she finally managed to track me down through friends in California. "It's got to be some kind of omen," she added. "Someone's telling you to quit running at night."

People who know me acknowledge, with rolling eyes, two things about me: I don't often have a given telephone number or address for long, and I love to run every night around 7 or 8—just before or long after sunset, depending on the season. It's past bedtime for babies in the car-size strollers that take up too much room in Riverside Park, hours after old ladies walk their yippy dogs on 50-foot leashes, long after the leering, beer-bellied men have gone home to sit in front of the TV. Finally, I can do my eight-mile, hour-long run without anyone getting in my way.

My friends look on in blank-faced dismay as I lace up my running shoes; they plead with me not to go. When I reach for my Walkman, it's the last straw; they tell me dryly that I might as well take along some ID, too.

I've tried to explain: I need my unencumbered daily runs the way others need therapy or sex or cigarettes. Once I could slip out the door with merely a shrug or sarcastic comment about how it's been nice knowing me. But since the body was found—even though it looks as if the woman's death had nothing to do with running late—the chorus of protests has been unrelenting. Friends, family, co-workers and the men who own the deli where I buy water every night after my run try to save me from myself.

And since the most recent rape in Central Park . . . the chorus has gotten louder. "Don't run after dark. Don't run alone. Don't run with your Walkman. Don't run where there's not much traffic. Don't run where there are no other people around. Don't run in Manhattan; join a gym. Don't stay in Manhattan; it's not safe." Even: "Come home to run in Sacramento, where it's safe."

I wonder, then, what kind of "omen" it was when on my last visit home I went for a run through my old suburban neighborhood and into the ritzier American River area. A jogger was raped that night not a mile from where I myself had turned back.

Everyone says I am "asking for it"—"it" being what happened to the woman who ended up in the trailer or to the woman from Sacramento. I'm not, of course, any more than I am asking for sexual harassment when I run in the light of day in shorts with my breasts encased in a running bra that fits like an Ace bandage. Sometimes it

gets so bad that I consider joining a gym. Sometimes I consider moving to a place where it's safe for a girl to run, or where it's safe to be a
girl, period.

But where would that be? Before the body was identified, it was
assumed the woman had been running at night. How foolish, we all
said, shaking our heads over the paper that morning. Now that it
seems that she might have been killed by an abusive ex-boyfriend, we
still blame her for her own violent death.

I had a roommate who once said I was a fool for wearing running
shorts with built-in underwear. "If you get raped, the defense attorney
could hold them up in court and say you were asking for it because
you weren't wearing any underwear," she said. At the time, I laughed.
Now, I'm thinking twice.

Having been mistaken for this woman has been both disturbing
and enlightening in an unexpected, *It's a Wonderful Life* way. Living in
a city that can make you feel as if you could drop off the face of the
earth and no one would notice, I am warmed by the discovery that
this isn't necessarily true. And I am jarred by the realization that not
only could the victim have been me but also that it could *be* me.

I Will Not Live Like a Victim

To start living like a victim to avoid becoming one is not the solution.
I have no intention of joining an expensive gym, finding a man or a
dog to run with, or scheduling my life by the rising and setting sun
like a defenseless heroine in an old horror movie. (The creature
always found a way to get at her, anyway.) My mother has long since
stopped warning me not to run at night and instead tells me to be
careful when I run at night—the kind of sensible advice a person can
live with.

A detective I talked to after the body was found wondered at the
fact that two nights later he saw a woman jogging after dark not two
blocks from where the police believed the murder occurred. "I guess
she hadn't heard about it," he said with a sigh.

Nah. She probably just figured that since violence is everywhere,
and since as a woman, she's the most likely to be its victim, there's no
place to hide. You might as well get on with your life in spite of it.

THE OTHER HALF OF SILENCE

Zachary, as told to Charlotte Pierce-Baker

Zachary is one of several men who was interviewed by author Charlotte Pierce-Baker for her book *Surviving the Silence: Black Women's Stories of Rape*. In the following excerpt from the book, Zachary recounts a time in his life when he was romantically involved with a woman who had been raped. He discusses the difficulties of this relationship, which was emotionally—but not physically—intimate. Although Zachary initially wanted to help this woman, his attempts at assistance seemed to fail, and a distance grew between them. However, he states, the two have remained friends, and he credits this friendship with making him more sensitive toward women.

I was about thirty-one or thirty-two, and Alice was twenty-four. I was single. Although Alice told me during the first period we dated that she had been raped, I had not remembered it. She told me again when we started dating a second time. She was upset that I had not remembered: "But I *told* you!" she said—as if I should have remembered. She had so much faith and trust in me, so my not understanding—my forgetting about her disclosure of rape—meant to her that I was unable to deal with who she had become.

Alice never got therapy after her rape. She had been on a date with her boyfriend. She was eighteen and at college. Someone hijacked them on the road in the small town where she was living. The man told her boyfriend to get in the trunk of the car. She said she would have fought him, but he threatened to kill her boyfriend if she didn't give him what he wanted. She doesn't remember how long they were out there in the woods. After he raped her, he let them go. She did not go to the hospital, but went back to the dorm. She told someone at the dorm; I don't know who. But I do know that there were no charges. *And* I know that the rapist came back looking for her. It was a small town and a small school. She said, "He came back for me!" She has brothers and she never told them or her parents.

How the Rape Affected Our Relationship

The rape had a lot to do with our relationship. It got in the way. I think it's one of the main reasons our relationship did not work. She did not want to touch or be touched. We slept together but we had no sex. I couldn't fulfill her notion of what a partner should be. Then the time came when I *did* want to have sex and she didn't. It changed the nature of the relationship. It was strange, but our sense of closeness had to do with our reluctance to talk about the rape. But still I kept going back and forth—we were a long distance apart—to see her even though we didn't sleep together. We had lots of common interests, and we still had a real sense of closeness. I think she felt safe with me because I had just separated from my long-time girlfriend; I didn't want or need to get involved sexually, and Alice didn't want to either—for different reasons. The fact that she had been raped had a lot to do with it. We looked good on paper, but the relationship didn't work.

When I first met Alice, I was pretty down on women and cynical since my girlfriend and I had just split up. I was in and out of dating relationships. Alice was probably the one person with whom a relationship was comfortable. We didn't expect anything of one another. And I found out very quickly with Alice that I had to tell and *do* the truth. I definitely couldn't play games with her. I had to be serious about what I said and did. What was uncomfortable was that I found out that *I* could fail her, and her other men couldn't. She was looking for success from me. Soon after we started seeing each other, I found out that she had invested so much in me, and she was expecting a return on the investment. I was just looking at the two of us as equals. She was sharing secrets with me. I was very special to her, but I didn't see it. When I realized it, it blew me away. The highs and lows of her—the unpredictability—I didn't understand. That I could fail her really didn't come to me 'til years later.

I Could Not Touch

After Alice told me of her rape, she became sacred to me. I could adore her. I could love her. I could not touch. She pushed me further away, even though I grew closer to *her*. It was an unsettling duality. I felt I was in the position of therapist. We'd talk for hours. She'd say, "Zach, I've shared *everything* with you, things no one else knows. I've been spiritually and mentally intimate with you. I can say anything to you, and you should be able to do the same with me." At first I couldn't give anything back. She placed a crown on my head, and it was too heavy to bear. I didn't want to be another man, another person to disappoint and fail her.

Then there came a period in her life when she would sleep with anyone—one-night stands—it didn't matter. She would say, "Fucking is one thing and intimacy is another. What I have with you is intimacy. I feel much closer to you than to the men I fucked. Making love is one thing, but being close to you is more special." That bothered me a great deal. I wondered if we *had* been physical if I would be someone she just "fucked." So we never had sex. That "specialness" has been preserved.

Her rape—violation—affected her, and I wanted to "minister" to her. I wanted to be the one to make it all better. Her call for "space" or for "closeness" was never clear. She didn't always know either. The more we got to know one another, the worse it got. Here was someone I loved, someone with whom I could be fulfilled. But because of the rape, she didn't want kids, and she didn't want to be married. Because of *those* two things, I didn't want to stay with her.

There was consistently more tenderness on my side, even when she *seemed* not to want it. Maybe it was all a mask. It was so confusing. She would say, "You should have said this; you should have done that." I couldn't seem to get it right for her. So I decided to keep a distance. That's what she *seemed* to need. I thought, I'll try to treat her more special, more sacred. She was not like other women. It was like she wanted me to treat her special and at the same time treat her like everybody else. So I began to settle in my own comfort zone where she was concerned. Instead of going toward the pain, I pulled away. I didn't know whether I could pay the price.

Still Friends

We still talk a few times a year. We found that we could still be friends. When we talk, I can still feel the pain, the anger, the bitterness. She still has never told anyone [else], and she swore me to silence. She's working now and going to school. I guess I thought I had handled the issue of her being raped by being celibate, but I've learned over the years that sexuality and rape are separate. I thought they were the same.

Alice has changed how I regard women in general. I see her as being courageous and strong. The frightened woman—the scared, wounded woman in back of the courageous warrior woman—has made me much more sensitive to other women. I had Alice pegged a certain way, but as the layers fell away, I learned more and more about her. When I have a son, as soon as he learns language, I will start teaching him about women and how to be soft. The macho ethic of the black community works against us. I have two nephews and someone told one of them, "You're crying like a girl." That's not good. Women are seen as victims, and men are not supposed to cry. And so we have women acting like victims, and men who are afraid to show their feelings. Without a doubt, knowing Alice has changed my life.

THE URGE TO HURT

Michael Ross

Michael Ross, a convicted rapist and serial killer, was on death row in Connecticut when he wrote the following selection. Ross fully confesses that he raped and murdered eight women in three states, but he maintains that he was suffering from paraphilia, a mental illness that compels men to perpetrate violent sexual activity repeatedly. After receiving medication for this disorder while in prison, Ross claims that his violent urges ceased, allowing him to experience genuine sorrow and remorse over his crimes. To avoid future tragedies, he argues, paraphiliac disorder must be correctly diagnosed and readily treated.

My name is Michael Ross. I am a condemned man on death row. When most people think of death row inmates, I'm the one they think of. I'm the worst of the worst, a serial killer responsible for the rape and murder of eight women in three states who has assaulted several others and stalked and frightened many more. I have never denied what I did and have fully confessed to my crimes. The only issue in my case was, and still is, my mental condition. For years I have been trying to prove that I am suffering from a mental illness that drove me to rape and kill, and that this mental illness made me physically unable to control my actions. I have met with little success.

So here I sit on death row, waiting for the judicial system to complete the tedious process that will likely result in my execution. Sometimes, when I close my eyes, I can envision the hundreds of people who are likely to gather outside the prison gates on that night. I can see them waving placards, drinking and rejoicing, and I can hear their cheers as my death is finally announced.

Paraphiliac Disorder

Who is Michael Ross? And what could possibly motivate a clearly intelligent individual, a Cornell University graduate, to commit such horrendous crimes? As you might expect, I have been examined by many psychiatric experts since my arrest in 1984. All of them, including the state's own expert psychiatric witness, diagnosed me as suffering from a paraphiliac mental disorder called "sexual sadism," which,

Reprinted from Michael Ross, "The Urge to Hurt," *Utne Reader*, July/August 1997. Reprinted with permission from the author.

in the experts' words, resulted in my compulsion "to perpetrate violent sexual activity in a repetitive way." These experts also agreed that my criminal conduct was the direct result of uncontrollable sexual impulses caused by my mental illness. The state's only hope of obtaining a conviction was to inflame the jury's emotions so that they would ignore any evidence of psychological impairment. In my particular case, that was quite easy to do, and the state succeeded in obtaining convictions and multiple death sentences.

What exactly is a paraphiliac mental disorder? It is very difficult to explain and understand—especially for the layperson (which, unfortunately for me, describes most jury members). Basically, I was plagued by repetitive thoughts, urges, and fantasies of the degradation, rape, and murder of women. These unwanted thoughts filled my mind when I was awake, and they were in my dreams when I slept. Imagine trying to control such urges day by day, hour by hour. Also try to imagine the hatred, loathing, and abhorrence that I developed toward myself when I ultimately failed. The best way to understand this problem is to remember a time when you had a catchy tune stuck in your mind. Even if you like the melody, the constant repetition becomes more than merely annoying. The harder you try to push that melody out of your mind, the louder and more persistent it becomes, driving you almost mad. Now replace that sweet little melody with noxious thoughts of physically and mentally degrading a woman, of raping her and strangling her. Now you can begin to understand what I had running wild in my head. And I think you can begin to understand me when I say that it is not something I wanted.

The Desire to Harm Women
The urge to hurt women could come over me at any time, at any place. Powerful, sometimes irresistible desires would well up for no apparent reason and with no warning. Even after my arrest—while I was facing capital charges—these urges continued. I remember one day being transported back to the county jail from a court appearance just prior to my trial. I was in the back of a sheriff's van in full restraints—handcuffs, leg irons, belly chain—when we passed a young woman walking along the road. I cannot begin to describe the intensity of feeling that enveloped me that day. I wanted . . . no, I *had* to get out of that van and go after her. The situation was ludicrous. (And later, back in my cell, I masturbated to a fantasy of what would have happened had I gotten hold of her.)

Even after I was sentenced to death, the urges persisted. One day, after seeing my psychiatrist, I was being escorted, without restraints, back to my cell by a young female correctional officer. When we got to a secluded stairwell, I suddenly felt this overwhelming desire to hurt her. I knew that I had to get out of that stairwell, and I ran out into the hallway. I'll never forget how she shouted at me and threatened to write a disciplinary report; she didn't have a clue. She never knew how close I came to attacking her, and possibly even killing her.

Freedom on Death Row

You would think that being sentenced to death and living in a maximum-security prison would curb such urges, but this illness defies rationality. I eventually found some relief. Almost three years after I came to death row, I started to receive weekly injections of an anti-androgen medication called Depo-Provera. Three years later, after some liver function trouble, I was switched to monthly Depo-Lupron injections, which I still receive. What these drugs did was significantly reduce my body's natural production of the male sex hormone—testosterone. For some reason, testosterone affects my mind differently than it does the average male. A few months after I started the treatment, my blood serum testosterone dropped below prepubescent levels. (It's currently 20; the normal range is 260 to 1,250.) As this happened, nothing less than a miracle occurred. My obsessive thoughts and fantasies began to diminish.

Having those thoughts is a lot like living with an obnoxious roommate. You can't get away because they're always there. What the Depo-Lupron does for me is to move that roommate down the hall to his own apartment. The problem is still there, but it's easier to deal with because it isn't always intruding into my everyday life. The medication has rendered the "monster within" impotent and banished him to the back of my mind. And while he can still mock me on occasion, he no longer controls me.

You cannot begin to imagine what a milestone this was in my life. A whole new world opened up to me. I had my mind back—a clear mind free of malevolent thoughts and urges. It sounds strange for a condemned man to speak of being free on death row, but that is the only word I can think of to describe the transformation I have undergone. That's not to say all is well. One result of all this was that I was forced to look at myself. I'm not talking the cursory, superficial manner in which most people look at themselves, but rather the painful, unrelenting search into the depths of my soul.

Many prison inmates are able to lie convincingly to themselves, to see themselves as basically good people who are innocent victims of an unfair and uncaring society. Sometimes it is very difficult to see ourselves as we truly are, and much easier to blame others for our actions. For years that is exactly what I did. I was angry at everyone except the person I should have been most angry with—myself. It took years for that anger to subside and for me to begin to accept what I had become.

Not only did the Depo-Lupron free my mind, it also allowed my moral judgment to awaken, which gave me back something that I thought I had lost forever—my humanity. Now that my mind was clear, I began to be aware of things I didn't like about myself. I realized how weak and afraid I really was, and how I had allowed the monster in my mind to control me. I began to feel the terrible agony and distress that I had caused my victims, their families and friends, my own family. I also began to feel the awesome weight of responsibility for my actions. And finally, I felt the profound sense of guilt that surrounds my soul with dark, tormented clouds of self-hatred and remorse. All of which leaves me with a deep desire to make amends, which, under the present circumstances, seems all but impossible. Yet it is what I yearn for the most: reconciliation with the spirits of my victims, with their families and friends, with myself and my God. If this happens it will be the final—and undoubtedly most difficult—part of my transformation. If only science could create a drug to help me with this problem.

One thing is surely true: There are other "Michael Rosses" out there in various stages of development who need a place where they can go for help. Society needs to ensure correct diagnosis and early treatment in the future. It's easy to point a finger at me, to call me evil and condemn me to death. But if that is all that happens, it will be a terrible waste. Tragic murders such as those I committed can be avoided in the future, but only if society stops turning its back, stops condemning, and begins to acknowledge and treat the problem. Only then will something constructive come out of the events that took the lives of eight women, left their families and friends bereaved, resulted in my incarceration and probable execution, and caused untold shame and anguish to my own family. The past has already happened. It's up to you to change the future.

CHAPTER 5

REDUCING AND PREVENTING RAPE

SOCIETY NEEDS BETTER LAWS AGAINST RAPE

Stephen Schulhofer

Despite decades of legal reforms, laws against rape and sexual assault remain largely ineffective in protecting women's sexual autonomy, writes Stephen Schulhofer in the following selection. In most states, unwanted sexual intercourse is not defined as rape unless the assailant uses certain kinds of physical force or threatens bodily injury, Schulhofer explains. Furthermore, he notes, a victim who does not physically resist because she is afraid or because she is under the influence of alcohol or drugs often cannot file criminal charges against her attacker under existing laws. Such legal barriers to justice must be challenged in order to secure everyone's right to set sexual boundaries, the author concludes. Schulhofer is a law professor at the University of Chicago and the author of *Unwanted Sex: The Culture of Intimidation and the Failure of Law*.

A young Illinois woman stopped to rest while biking along an isolated reservoir near the town of Carbondale. A stranger approached and struck up a conversation. After chatting with him for a few minutes, she got on her bicycle and started to leave. At that point the man, Joel Warren, put his hand on her shoulder. When she said, "No, I have to go now," he replied, "This will only take a minute. My girlfriend doesn't meet my needs." He added, "I don't want to hurt you."

Perhaps Warren only meant "We'll both enjoy this." But to the woman his comment sounded ominous, a hint of what he might do if she resisted him. In any event she had little time to consider nuances. Warren quickly lifted her up and carried her into the woods. He was six feet three inches tall and weighed 185 pounds. With no one else in sight, the young woman, who was only five feet two and weighed 100 pounds, did not attempt to scream or fight back, actions that she feared might prompt him to start choking or beating her. Once Warren had her hidden from view, he pulled off her pants, pushed up her shirt to expose her breasts, and subjected her to several acts of oral sex.

The police eventually identified Warren, prosecutors charged him

Excerpted from Stephen Schulhofer, "Unwanted Sex," *The Atlantic Monthly*, October 1998. Copyright © 1998 President and Fellows of Harvard College. Reprinted with permission from the publisher, Harvard University Press, Cambridge, MA.

with sexual assault, and a jury found him guilty. Yet an Illinois court set aside the conviction, saying that "the record is devoid of any attendant circumstances which suggest that complainant was compelled to submit." The year was 1983, but the court's approach remains very much with us.

Ineffective Laws

Despite decades of public discussion and numerous statutory reforms before and since decisions like this one, the problem of defining and protecting our sexual boundaries has not been solved. The reasons are many. Sometimes statutes are highly protective but ineffectively enforced. Whatever the law may say, jurors often assume that it is neither abnormal nor harmful for a man to make aggressive physical advances to a silent, passive, or openly reluctant woman—literally to sweep her off her feet, pull off her clothes, and penetrate her, all without any explicit indication of her consent. Some jurors assume that women who submit to these advances really want the sexual contact, that they could easily resist if they didn't, or that it would be unfair to punish a man who, after all, was only doing what (so they may think) nature intended.

But attitudes like these are no longer universal. Our sexual culture has changed. Prosecutors sometimes file charges and juries sometimes convict in cases that would have been laughed out of court twenty or thirty years ago. Yet the law itself continues to pose obstacles, blocking enforcement and denying remedies even when juries are prepared to condemn defendants' conduct as outrageous. With its many gaps and limits, the law even tends to validate and reinforce the strands within our culture that persist in seeing aggressive male sexuality as a biological given that poses no problems. Outmoded standards are especially evident in criminal law, but other remedies have many of the same failings.

Criminal law's most obvious weak spot is its continuing vagueness— a surprise after all the effort devoted to reform. Standards remain extraordinarily murky, especially for determining when a man's behavior amounts to prohibited force or when a woman's conduct signals her consent. And where criminal law is murky, the benefit of the doubt usually goes to the defendant, in theory and often in practice. Acquittal rates are not noticeably lower for rape than they are for other serious felonies, but vague standards take their toll in other ways—deterring prosecutors from pursuing charges and deterring victims from filing complaints.

The number of cases affected is difficult to estimate, but a 1992 survey by researchers at the University of Chicago provides a chilling perspective on the problem. The survey found that 22 percent of American women felt they had been forced to have sex, yet only three percent of American men said they had ever forced a woman to have sex. After discounting the possibility that the men or the women had lied, or that a few men were responsible for forcing many different women, the researchers concluded that most of the men simply did not realize that their sexual partners were unwilling. The researchers wrote, "There seems to be not just a gender gap but a gender chasm in perceptions of when sex was forced."

Criminal Law's Definition of Consent

But criminal-law rules are sometimes quite clear—especially when they *exclude* certain kinds of abuse. In the fall of 1988 a young Montana woman wrote an alarming letter to her school board. She claimed that two years earlier, during her senior year in high school, the school's principal had forced her to submit to intercourse by threatening to block her graduation. After an investigation by the county prosecutor, the principal was charged with two acts of "sexual intercourse without consent," a felony under Montana law.

Like many other cases of rape, indecent assault, or sexual harassment, the Montana case bristled with credibility questions. But the Montana Supreme Court decided that the victim's story, even if true, could not support criminal charges. In Montana, as in most states, a sexual-assault charge normally requires proof that the abuser used physical force or threatened the victim with physical injury. Submission to avoid other kinds of harm is not enough to meet the statutory requirement of intercourse "without consent." The court itself was appalled by the narrow scope of the statute. The judges dismissed the case "with a good deal of reluctance," noting their "strong condemnation of the alleged acts," and adding, "If we could rewrite the statutes to [punish] the alleged acts . . . we would willingly do so."

In a situation like the one in Montana, the victim has a hard choice to make. An exceptionally self-possessed young woman might just tell her principal to get lost. But if she submits to the man's sexual demands, then as far as criminal law is concerned, she has consented.

Rape laws have moved far since the days when women were required to resist "to the utmost." Today "reasonable" resistance is supposed to be sufficient. In the more progressive states no resistance is required at all. But in nearly all states intimidation short of physical threats is still treated as if it were mere "persuasion." When it succeeds, courts will usually say that the victim "consented."

The Required Kind of Force

We have all heard of cases in which the police, judge, or jury refused to believe that a woman's "no" really meant no. But the problems run deeper: even when jurors are convinced that a woman was unwilling, unwillingness is not enough. In the face of clearly expressed objections, intercourse is still not considered rape or any other form of felonious assault unless the assailant used physical force or threatened bodily injury. And the law's definition of physical force remains extremely strict. The physical acts of lifting a woman up or pushing her onto a bed and accomplishing sexual penetration usually aren't enough. The "force" must be something beyond the acts involved in intercourse— something that physically "compels" the woman to submit.

Because nearly all states require proof of physical force in prosecutions for rape or sexual assault, many serious abuses are classified as "nonviolent" and penal sanctions are assumed to be inappropriate. The abuses are not really nonviolent, of course. It is more accurate to say that they don't involve what the law regards as the *required kind* of force. The force they do involve is seen as normal and therefore permissible.

When men use only the "right kind" of force, prosecutors seldom bother to file charges. But sometimes such cases are brought to court, often because of an aggravating element such as the youth of the victim. When prosecutors bring these cases, judges usually take the occasion to remind them that the force requirement will be strictly observed.

In a 1982 Mississippi case a fourteen-year-old girl I will call Sally was visiting her married sister, Elizabeth, who had recently separated from her husband, Dennis McQueen. One day Dennis stopped by Elizabeth's house and asked to take their two-year-old baby for a ride in his truck. Elizabeth did not want to leave Dennis alone with the baby, so she asked Sally to go along. When they returned, Sally was shaking and crying. She told her sister that Dennis had pulled off onto a deserted road and told her to get out of the truck. He told her to take off her clothes, lie down on the front seat, and put her legs up on his shoulders. Sally explained that she was scared of him because he had been drinking, and was afraid he was going to hurt her. She said she complied, crying throughout, as Dennis penetrated her and quickly had intercourse.

Because Mississippi then set the age of consent for intercourse at fourteen, Dennis McQueen was not charged with statutory rape. He was prosecuted for forcible rape, and the jury found him guilty. But the Mississippi Supreme Court set aside the conviction, because McQueen "did not threaten to injure [Sally], did not forcibly remove her from the truck, did not remove her clothes, and did not forcibly make her lie down in the truck." In 1992 an Ohio court reversed a similar conviction, invoking the same principle: no proof of physical force.

When the victim is only fourteen, most states would be able to charge a man like McQueen with statutory rape. In 1998 Mississippi raised its age of consent—to sixteen. But when a young woman reaches the age of sixteen, or in some states eighteen, statutory-rape charges are no longer possible; the man is likely to escape any criminal sanction.

Unwanted Sexual Demands

The narrow scope of contemporary criminal law becomes especially significant when a woman confronts sexual pressure from a man who holds professional power over her. Women face recurrent sexual demands from teachers, job supervisors, psychotherapists, doctors, and lawyers who misuse their authority to compel sexual submission. The best available estimates suggest that each year roughly a million working women are pressured to have sex with their job supervisors, and thousands (probably hundreds of thousands) of college women face unwanted sexual demands from their professors. Thousands more women submit each year to unwanted sex with their psychotherapists and physicians. Yet rape law offers no help in these situations, because the tactics the men use, though sometimes flagrantly coercive, are not physically violent. And civil suits, along with administrative penalties, often prove ineffective as well. Men who abuse their status or professional authority to coerce sexual compliance often face no significant sanctions.

Karen (not her real name), the mother of three children, sought legal help to escape a troubled marriage. She hired a lawyer and paid him a $2,500 retainer. Later, distraught and insecure, she went to see him to discuss her case. He locked his office door, unzipped his pants, and asked her for oral sex. Convinced that he would drop her case and abandon her if she refused, Karen complied, and on two later occasions she submitted to his demands for intercourse. After several months she could no longer cope with the lawyer's sexual demands. She fired him and sued for malpractice. But in a 1990 decision an Illinois court said that she had no case, even if the lawyer had exploited her vulnerability and used his professional position to coerce her consent. The court ruled that lawyers can be held accountable for malpractice only when their misconduct has an adverse effect on their clients' *legal* problems. Emotional harm from coerced submission to repugnant sexual demands was, the court said, "insufficient"; the woman had no case because she "did not claim that her legal position in the divorce proceedings was harmed."

Resistance Requirements?

Alcohol can add another dimension to the problem. A widely reported 1996 trial involved a woman in upstate New York who had been drinking heavily on a date and passed out in a restaurant bathroom. Her date, waiting for her outside, fell asleep in his pickup truck. Meanwhile, five men carried the woman from the bathroom to a booth, where they undressed her. All five then allegedly raped her, left her in the booth, and returned to their beer and sandwiches.

The five men admitted the acts of intercourse, pleaded guilty to minor misdemeanor charges, and were fined $840 each. But after a political uproar over the leniency of the sentences, a special prosecutor managed to get the guilty pleas set aside and brought the first of the defendants to trial on felony rape charges. At the trial, the *New York Times* reported, the man's lawyer argued that "if the woman had consumed enough alcohol to be helpless, as she testified, then she could not be sure that she had not consented to sex." He didn't say, of course, that the men should be sure that she *had* consented. Genuine willingness on the part of the woman simply isn't required. The jury acquitted the man.

Criminal-law reforms often leave a false impression. For example, resistance requirements have supposedly been restricted or abolished. But when a woman says no, clearly and insistently, a man can still roll on top of her, remove her clothes, and penetrate her, all without committing rape. The obstacle in such a case is not conflicting versions of the truth or questions of credibility. The man can admit to the facts, more or less with impunity. His conduct remains perfectly legal, because he has not used what the law calls force—that is, physical power *in addition to* the force that may be intrinsic to intercourse.

The upshot is that resistance requirements remain in effect even where the law says they have been abolished. A woman's right to bodily integrity and sexual autonomy—her right to sexual choice—simply does not exist until she begins to scream or fight back physically.

Sexual-Harassment Laws

Sexual-harassment suits provide an alternative for women who are coerced by tactics that stop short of physical force. It would be natural to assume that sexual-harassment laws fill the gap left by criminal law's strict force requirement, because these laws are so often portrayed as exceedingly restrictive. Vocal critics of these laws imply that they impose draconian sanctions on any man who dares to use off-color language or express the slightest hint of sexual interest in the presence of an exceptionally sensitive woman. In fact sexual-harassment laws do nothing of the kind. On the contrary, they remain limited in their coverage and effectiveness.

With few exceptions, sexual-harassment laws, state and federal, extend protection only to employees and students. They are no help at all when a patient is pressured for sex by her doctor or when a client in a divorce proceeding is coerced by a lawyer who threatens to stop working on her case if she won't meet his sexual demands.

Even in the workplace, sexual-harassment laws are at best only partly effective. The laws apply if a supervisor or a professor is stupid enough to tell a woman that he will hurt her career unless she submits to him. But sexual-harassment laws often ignore the pressure that lurks beneath the surface of sexual demands from a professor or a job supervisor. And even when an explicit threat can be proved, remedies are limited. The law permits civil damage suits against universities and companies, and such suits are often well publicized. What is less well known is that even when clear abuses are committed, the offender isn't personally liable for damages; sexual-harassment penalties apply only against the university or the business as an entity.

A series of Supreme Court decisions in 1998 made clear that women subjected to sexual harassment can sue even when they have not been fired or denied a promotion. But at the same time the Court created new defenses that will permit many corporations and school districts to escape responsibility for harassment by their employees, and it left in place the rule that the employees themselves are not personally liable. President Bill Clinton's position in the Paula Jones suit is an exception, because a public official can be sued personally, under a separate set of federal laws, if he or she uses governmental power to violate a citizen's civil rights. However, the ordinary supervisor or teacher who uses his position to gain sexual favors usually incurs no civil or criminal liability, even for acts blatantly interfering with the sexual autonomy of a subordinate.

A Daunting Task

This gap in the law is puzzling, but not simple to fill. It is a daunting task to define, clearly and specifically, what an appropriate system for protection of sexual autonomy should look like. It is not easy to set the boundaries for permissible conduct when positions of authority, threats, promises, alcohol, and abuses of trust have some effect on sexual interaction.

A prison guard's power clearly prevents an inmate from choosing freely whether to accept or refuse a sexual proposal, but do we say the same about a college professor and a nineteen-year-old student taking his course? Do we say the same about a corporate vice-president and a junior executive working in another division? There are problems in such relationships, to be sure. But if sexual interaction is ruled legally out of bounds every time one of the parties has any possible source of power over the other, our opportunities to find companionship and sexual intimacy will shrink drastically. To create a legal barrier to every relationship not formed on the purely neutral ground of the singles bar or the church social would be pathetic and absurd.

A woman too drunk to stand up should not be expected to resist physically or to protest explicitly—even if she downed all the drinks of her own accord and knew exactly what was in them. But do we say the same about a woman who has had just two or three drinks? Should we conclude that a woman's consent is invalid if she said "yes" because she was feeling relaxed and uninhibited after drinking a glass of wine? The law's willingness to find consent in cases of severe alcohol impairment should be considered intolerable, but a standard suggesting that rape occurred whenever alcohol played a part in sexual consent would be intolerable as well.

Sexual Autonomy

Respect for sexual autonomy requires safeguards against abuse and exploitation. But—equally important—it requires that the law protect our freedom to seek emotional intimacy and sexual fulfillment with willing partners. Despite decades of discussion and years of ambitious feminist reforms, adequate protection of sexuality remains elusive, in part because freedom from unwanted sex and the freedom to seek mutually desired sex sometimes seem to be in tension. A workable notion of sexual autonomy appears to require compromises and balancing—the kind of chore that lawyers and academics often regard as a technical problem of "line-drawing." But the problem is neither simple nor unimportant. What is at stake is nothing less than women's bodily security and every person's right to control the boundaries of his or her own sexual experience. . . .

Sexual autonomy, like other rights, has two facets. The first is active—the right to decide on the kind of life one wishes to live and the kinds of activities one wishes to pursue, including sexual interaction with others who are willing. The second is the reverse—the right to safeguard and exclude, the freedom to refuse to have sex with any person at any time, for any reason or for no reason at all.

Protection from coercion and the protection of autonomy are closely related and thus sometimes hard to tell apart. Existing rape laws and all the leading reform efforts add to this confusion by treating the two concerns as if they were two sides of the same coin. But the differences between them are crucial. Physical coercion interferes with autonomy, but many interferences with autonomy involve no coercion, physical or otherwise. . . .

The Silence-Means-Consent Assumption

Courts that find consent despite a verbal protest will inevitably find consent if the woman didn't protest or physically resist. But even courts and juries that treat a verbal no as sufficient to signal unwillingness are likely to consider a woman's silence equivalent to consent. Only a handful of states have taken the next step and insisted that consent to sex requires "affirmative and freely given permission." To most courts, a refusal to infer consent when a woman lies still and utters no protest is overly fastidious and wildly unrealistic. If a woman is unconscious or asleep, of course, her silence can't be equated with sexual willingness; a man who penetrates her will be guilty of rape. But when the woman is *able* to say no, the usual assumption is that if she remains silent, she must be willing; otherwise she would object. Or if she isn't really willing, it is considered fair to treat her as if she were. Consent may be actual, or it may be a justified fiction. The episode on the Illinois bike path is just one of countless illustrations of this point of view. The court that reversed the man's sexual-assault conviction said that the woman's "failure to resist when it was within her power to do so conveys the impression of consent."

The soundness of requiring some protest is usually accepted without question. Yet it is by no means clear that women in such situations do have a fair chance to protest. The Illinois woman, for example, was a foot shorter and weighed eighty-five pounds less than her attacker, and was startled by a stranger in an isolated setting, with no one else in sight. Her silence might mean enthusiastic willingness, but it is *at least* equally likely that she was terrified and paralyzed by fear.

The silence-means-consent assumption draws support even from some rape-law reformers. They worry that treating passivity or ambivalence as nonconsent will patronize women, who should be assumed to be capable of asserting their own wishes. But we seldom think it patronizing to insist on permission, not just silence, when the interests affected are ones that men can easily recognize. When a doctor asks if a patient wants a probe inserted into his rectum to check for tumors, the patient's silence is not assumed to indicate consent. The patient's willingness must be made explicit. Yet rape law doesn't require us to obtain actual permission for intercourse; it prohibits penetration only when there is clear evidence of *non*consent.

An insistence on proof of unwillingness has a certain logic within the framework of existing law. It serves not only to ensure that potential lawbreakers have fair warning but also to keep the criminal prohibition focused on conduct involving force. A requirement of actual permission, however, would not shift the burden of proof to the defendant or require doubts to be resolved against him. A defendant could be convicted only if he knew he did not have the woman's affirmative permission or if he was criminally negligent in thinking that he did. But silence, ambiguous behavior, and the absence of a clearly expressed preference would be evidence that affirmative consent was absent; they would no longer suggest, as they do under present law, that a defendant did nothing wrong in forging ahead to intercourse. . . .

The Law Must Be Changed

The central point is that sexual intimacy must be chosen freely. The first priorities are to stop insisting on proof of the woman's opposition, and to stop requiring her to take actions clear enough to overcome the law's presumption that she is always interested in sex—at any time, in any place, with any person. The legal standard must move away from the demand for unambiguous evidence of her protests and insist instead that the man have affirmative indications that she chose to participate. So long as her choice is clearly expressed, by words or conduct, her right to control her sexuality is respected.

These important steps are not sufficient by themselves, however. In states that now require affirmative, "freely given" consent, the law still makes no effort to define which kinds of pressure prevent consent from being given "freely." Experience under New Jersey's relatively progressive rule has demonstrated that when the concepts of force and coercion are left undefined, prosecutors continue to insist on evidence of physical intimidation. The law must stop equating force with physical violence.

Without this change of focus, clear-cut abuses will continue to slip through the gaps in existing law. Men today are free, as in the Illinois case, to take advantage of strangers they accost in isolated settings. Lawyers in most states can exact sexual cooperation from clients who depend on them for essential help in divorce, child-custody, and criminal cases. A man in a bar or a fraternity house can get a woman drunk, undress her, and penetrate her before she can resist. In cases like these men continue to escape conviction by claiming that they never threatened physical violence and that the woman failed to make her unwillingness clear. Only when our laws and culture acknowledge the importance of affirmative, uncoerced permission will we afford women and men the right to control the boundaries of their own sexual lives. Until then sexual autonomy will remain the missing, unprotected entitlement.

How to Spot and Resist Acquaintance Rapists

Susan Jacoby

In the following selection, New York writer Susan Jacoby presents strategies for avoiding acquaintance rape. Fending off such an assault poses special difficulties, writes Jacoby, because it can be difficult to recognize that an acquaintance or friend is a threat until he actually attempts the rape. Moreover, she points out, women are often reluctant to appear rude, to scream, or to run away when a sexual assailant is someone they know. Citing recommendations from interviews with rape victims, researchers, and police officers, Jacoby advises women to be less trusting and more assertive and defensive when they find themselves in situations conducive to acquaintance rape.

Alexandra [not her real name], a 26-year-old graduate student at Harvard University, was delighted when an old friend turned up in Boston on a business trip. He called her from the airport, and she invited him over for coffee at her apartment.

An hour later, Alexandra was stunned when the man tried to kiss her as she brewed coffee in the kitchen. "He was a friend of my former boyfriend, so I knew him quite well, but there had never been anything romantic between us," she says. "Here he was, all over me, telling me there was nothing standing between us now that John, my ex, was out of the picture. Before I could think what to do—before I'd really taken in what was going on—he was ripping my blouse."

Realizing that she was in danger of being raped, Alexandra screamed loudly, over and over again. Her neighbors phoned the campus police, and officers arrived in less than five minutes—in time to pound on the door and stop the attack.

Alexandra emerged from the experience shaken and bruised, but she was lucky. In the jargon of crime statistics, she was a "rape avoider" rather than a rape victim. She's especially lucky, experts say, because she avoided rape even though she knew her assailant and was in a closed apartment—two factors that reduce the likelihood that a woman will successfully fend off a sexual assault.

The Difficulties in Resisting Acquaintance Rape

Most specialists agree that women face extra psychological difficulties in resisting a sexual assailant they know. That's an alarming suggestion in view of the fact that a very high percentage of adult rape attempts are by a man who was known to the victim before the crime, according to many experts. (Approximately 70 percent of adult victims of completed rapes know their assailants, according to the National Women's Study, considered the most accurate survey on rape.)

"As police officers who talk to lots of women crime victims, we constantly see that there are special problems involved in resisting acquaintance rape," says Sergeant Susan Morley, commanding officer of the New York Police Department's Special Victims Liaison Squad. "With a stranger, a woman usually realizes she's in danger at an earlier point. But if the assailant is your brother-in-law bringing over baked ziti for the party you're throwing that night, your alarm bells just don't start ringing right away."

Even when the alarm bells do ring, many women targeted by acquaintances are too embarrassed to use strategies that would increase their chances of escape. In a survey funded by the National Institute of Mental Health (NIMH), researchers compared resistance strategies used by victims of stranger and acquaintance rape.

The study found that the behavior of women attacked by acquaintances differed significantly in two ways from that of women assaulted by strangers. Acquaintance-rape victims were much less likely to scream for help. Only 11 percent did so, compared with more than 31 percent of stranger-rape victims. And only half as many of the acquaintance-rape victims tried to run away.

The study also showed that an almost identical proportion of women, nearly 70 percent, put up a physical struggle, regardless of whether they were attacked by strangers or acquaintances—evidence that acquaintance rape is not just a "misunderstanding" between flirting partners. Unfortunately, by the time victims start to fight, it may be too late.

Mary P. Koss, Ph. D., a professor of family and community medicine at the University of Arizona College of Medicine and the principal investigator of the NIMH survey, points out that research over the past twenty years has shown that screaming and running, as opposed to struggling, are the strategies most likely to lead to avoidance of rape. Koss acknowledges that the NIMH study included only women who *were* victims of completed rapes, but says, "Many women will be raped by a stronger man regardless of what they do to resist, and we know that sometimes a woman cries for help and no one responds. But not crying out *guarantees* that no one will come to your aid."

To develop better rape-avoidance radar, Sergeant Morley of the NYPD suggests that women stop equating date rape with acquaintance rape. "The public tends to think of all acquaintance rapes as growing out of a sexually ambiguous dating situation," she notes. "That often *is* the case. But acquaintance rapists run the gamut from a date to a friend to the guy you see around the neighborhood who asks to use the phone or the colleague at work who offers you a ride home.

"Different factors come into play in different situations. You can just say no to the guy who asks to use the phone. But what about the friend who's already in your house?"

A breakdown of adult rape cases from the National Women's Study shows that the largest single group of acquaintance rapists—accounting for 20 percent of all rape cases—were described by women simply as friends. Friends were followed by husbands (16 percent) and boyfriends (14 percent). Approximately 9 percent of all rapes were committed by nonrelatives such as handymen, neighbors or coworkers.

Pauline Bart, Ph.D., a professor in the Department of Psychiatry at the University of Illinois at Chicago and a pioneering researcher in the field, says that the wide variety of acquaintance rapes contributes to the difficulty of prevention: "If you look at the full range of men who rape women they know, you'd advise a woman never to accept a ride home with a man, never to invite a man in for coffee, never to go to his apartment. That would be a paranoid way of life.

"But there's an important line between paranoia and reasonable self-protection, and usually women draw that line too close for security," Bart adds. "To reduce vulnerability to acquaintance rape, we have to talk about moving that line further away. Being alert to potential danger isn't paranoid—it's prudent."

Every rape-prevention expert emphasizes that there is no surefire formula for avoiding sexual assault—and that no woman should blame herself for a rape if her strategy didn't work. But they also emphasize that all acquaintance rapes begin with a man who takes advantage of a woman who trusts him too much.

According to Bart, "On some level, the acquaintance rapist is always a man who has tricked you into thinking you're safe with him. To reduce the incidence of this trickery—you can't prevent it altogether—women do have to school themselves to be less trusting and nice." Specifically, that means following the guidelines below.

Trust Your Early-Warning Instincts

"This is the biggest piece of advice we can safely give all women," says Sergeant Morley. "We police officers can't say to women that they *should* scream—because suppose a guy already has his hands on your throat? Every dangerous situation is different. But we *can* say that you should not—must not—ignore the little inner voice that tells you something is wrong. A lot of women don't listen to that voice. Instead they tell themselves, 'Don't be silly, it's just good old Joe.'"

Detective Dianne Cruz Licata, also with the NYPD's Special Victims Liaison Squad, points out that many women comply with male requests that make them uncomfortable because they don't want to appear overly suspicious. "Okay, you can be wrong in your feeling that something's a little off. But what's the worst that can happen if you are being too suspicious? The worst is that you'll feel a little foolish. But the worst that can happen if your instincts were right and you didn't take action is that you get raped."

Ask Elena [not her real name], a 22-year-old market researcher who accepted a ride home from a male colleague. "His apartment was on the way to my apartment, and he said he wanted to stop at his place and change clothes because he had a date that night and the woman lived closer to me. I said I'd wait for him in the lobby of his building, but he kept urging me to come up.

"I began to feel suspicious because it seemed to me he was making too much of a fuss. He said, 'Come on, you don't want my neighbors to think I'm the kind of guy who leaves a girl standing in the lobby.'

"I wasn't thinking about rape—I just felt I wasn't comfortable going to the apartment of a man I hardly knew. But I also felt unsophisticated, so I went along. He locked the door and raped me immediately when we got inside, saying, 'You stupid cunt, you came up here on your own, that's why you're not going to tell anyone.'"

Elena did report the rape, but the man pleaded guilty to a lesser assault charge and served just six months in jail.

"There was a moment when I had a choice," Elena says, "and I made the wrong one. I'm not saying I'm responsible for being raped— only that it wouldn't have happened if I'd done what I wanted to do and stayed in that lobby.

"I would say to the woman who does have a moment of choice: Have the courage to look silly. What if the guy does think you're acting like a little girl? Who cares what he thinks? No man's opinion is more important than your safety."

Don't Be Afraid to Be Rude

For many women, acting on early-warning instincts means overcoming an ingrained reluctance to appear rude.

"If you have the slightest inkling that something isn't right," says Sergeant Morley, "the thing that you have to tell yourself is that *you don't owe this guy a thing*. Maybe he will feel bad if you won't come up to his apartment. But it isn't your responsibility to make a man feel comfortable at all times."

Janet [not her real name], 30, the divorced mother of a 6-year-old, says she felt like "the worst bitch in the world" when she refused to let the father of one of her son's friends into her home at 9:00 one evening.

"He'd taken the boys to a baseball game that afternoon," she recalls, "and he said his son had left a favorite toy truck at my house. Something about this didn't sit right with me. I hadn't seen the toy truck. In any case, I wondered why he hadn't just called and asked me about it instead of driving over at night.

"Then I thought, 'Oh, you're being ridiculous making that man stand out on your porch.' But I don't have any nearby neighbors and I felt really vulnerable. I looked quickly around the living room and said, 'Sorry, no truck.' I felt incredibly rude. But then he said something in a very angry tone that made me realize I'd been 100 percent right: 'I can't believe you won't let me in your house. Score another one for paranoid feminism.' I could see him glaring at me through the window of the door, which I then double-locked. It was hard, very hard. My mother didn't raise me to be rude to the fathers of my child's friends."

A year later, Janet read in the newspaper that the man had been charged in an attempted rape by a secretary in the firm where he worked.

Run—Whether or Not You Are Fully Dressed

"It's very sad, but some women get raped because the disarray of their clothing embarrasses them into staying put," says rape researcher Pauline Bart.

Miranda [not her real name], a 20-year-old college junior, was nearly raped by a date in the parking lot of her Miami apartment.

"It was after our third date, at about one o'clock in the morning, and we were kissing in his car," she recalls. "When he tried to unhook my bra, I told him no, very clearly. He tore the strap, and I screamed—but he put his hand over my mouth and then ripped my skirt and shirt right off me. He just leaned back and laughed and said, 'We can take our time now; you're not going anywhere without anything on.'"

At that moment, Miranda says, she realized the car door was unlocked and she might be able to make a successful dash to the lobby of her building. "He wasn't even holding me down—he was that confident," she says. "In a split second, I thought about what the doorman would think when he saw me with nothing on but my panties. But I jumped out, ran, screamed and got the doorman's attention. He *did* laugh when he saw me, and I felt humiliated. But I didn't get raped."

Experts say Miranda's experience illustrates one common date-rape scenario: A woman is kissing or petting without intending to go further; the man treats her actions as foreplay and, despite her resistance, takes advantage of an isolated setting to attempt a rape.

Use Alcohol Moderately

Studies have shown that in roughly half of all acquaintance rapes, both the woman and the man were drinking. That percentage is possibly much higher for rapes that occur on dates, at parties, or in other social situations that commonly feature alcohol consumption.

"Unfortunately, for a woman, one of the consequences of having a few too many with the wrong person can be getting raped," says Sergeant Morley. Alcohol and drugs blunt warning instincts.

"Even if the woman is sober, there's danger when a man is drinking heavily. We know that alcohol goes along with all sorts of violent crimes—not just rape—committed by young men."

Bart, who discusses rape prevention with her students, says the rape-alcohol connection poses a particular danger for young women, who may not be accustomed to drinking or understand alcohol's effects on their minds and bodies.

"It's hard to talk about this with young women without sounding like Mom," she says. "The use of alcohol on dates and at parties permeates our culture, but older people are more apt to know their limits. Restricting alcohol consumption has to be a part of any reasonable woman's regular routine for protecting herself."

Shana [not her real name], a 21-year-old senior at the University of Chicago, agrees. In December 1993, Shana went to a party at her date's all-male residence. Her date—with whom she'd been out only twice before—tried to make her drink Scotch.

"I absolutely hate hard liquor," she says, "and I told him so. He kept saying no, no, wine won't do it for you—and my reaction was to stop drinking altogether. Everyone around me was getting drunk.

"I saw one guy trying to pull a woman into a bedroom, and that's when my warning beeper went off. I tried to get my date to take me home and he got quite angry. It was a sub-twenty-degree Chicago night, and he said if I wasn't going to be any fun, I could walk the two miles home alone. So I did."

When she returned from holiday break, Shana ran into another woman who had been at the party that night. "She started to cry when she saw me, and she kept saying that I was so lucky," she recalls. "She and another woman had been raped by three men."

Shana urged the woman to report the rapes and told her she would testify about the atmosphere she had observed at the party. "She wouldn't report it," Shana says. "Over and over, she kept saying my testimony wouldn't be any help because I had left—and if I left, the police would say she should have left too. I'm sure if I'd had a lot to drink, I wouldn't have been alert to the bad vibes either."

Report—Even If You Get Away

When Alexandra, the Harvard graduate student, escaped from her would-be rapist, she decided not to press charges—even though the campus police were on the scene, her neighbors had heard her screaming, and she had the bruises and torn clothing as proof of her struggle.

"I was just so grateful that I was all right, that he hadn't succeeded," she says. "I thought only about wanting to put what happened out of my mind. As time has gone by, I've had second thoughts. This man still calls me on the phone and acts as if *nothing happened.* He even asked if he could stay at my apartment overnight when he was in town and was surprised when I said, 'Are you out of your mind?'

"I understand now what I didn't then—that he has no sense of having done anything wrong. He probably tells himself it was just a misunderstanding. And now comes the question that makes me lose sleep. By not reporting this to the authorities, did I encourage him to think he could do this to other women?"

Law enforcement officials say Alexandra's behavior is common among women attacked by acquaintances.

"All types of rapes are underreported. Acquaintance rapes are reported less often than stranger rapes, and attempted acquaintance rapes even less often than that," says Sergeant Morley. "Acquaintance rapists rely on the victim's embarrassment. It's almost a given that when a victim is attacked by a man she knows, he'll say during the assault, 'You're not going to tell anyone. No one would believe you if you did.'"

Police departments across the nation encourage women to report rapes—and attempted rapes—as soon as possible. "It would be a lie to tell acquaintance-rape victims that getting a conviction will be easy," says Sergeant Morley. "You just don't know what juries are going to do, even though the public is becoming better educated. But one thing we do know: The sooner the crime is reported, the better the chance of conviction."

Authorities acknowledge that pressing charges can be time-consuming and emotionally grueling for the victim. But they say that it's extremely important for women to report attempted rapes even if they were lucky enough to get away. "The next woman may not be so lucky," says the NYPD's Detective Cruz Licata. "And women have to realize that there's a very high incidence of repeat offenders.

"When a woman is intimidated into silence because she's ashamed of having been taken in by a man she knows, the guy is going to try it with another woman. Reporting the crime is the best way to protect not just yourself but *all* women. It isn't easy—but it's vital."

Protecting Communities from Repeat Sex Offenders

Matthew Purdy

In the following selection, *New York Times* staff writer Matthew
Purdy reports on the recent wave of new laws intended to protect communities from sex criminals who have completed their
prison terms. Since released rapists and pedophiles have been
known to re-offend, he says, the government has enacted a law
requiring communities to be notified when a convicted sex
offender moves into a neighborhood. In addition, several states
have passed laws requiring the commitment of sex criminals to
mental hospitals after their release from prison, writes Purdy.
Supporters maintain that these state laws will protect society
from recidivist sex offenders, Purdy explains, but opponents
argue that such measures unfairly impose additional punishment
on people who have already served their sentences.

The campaign to tighten the noose on sex offenders by notifying
communities of their release from prison has intensified with a new
legislative assault on pedophiles and rapists. This one is intended to
keep the most dangerous of them from getting back on the streets in
the first place.

Going beyond the notification measures prompted by the Megan
Kanka case, a handful of states have enacted laws giving officials the
power to commit violent sex offenders to mental hospitals involuntarily once their prison terms are up—a strategy that employs civil
laws after criminal ones are exhausted. [Seven-year-old Megan Kanka
was raped and murdered in 1994 by a twice-convicted child molester.
"Megan's Law," enacted in 1996, requires that residents be informed
when a convicted sex offender moves into a neighborhood.]

In the last few years, more than 250 sex offenders have been committed to mental hospitals. And the movement to confine those who
are considered most likely to strike again is expected to spread across
the country with a Supreme Court decision in June 1997 upholding
Kansas' law allowing the involuntary commitment of people found
mentally abnormal and likely to commit a violent sex crime.

Reprinted from Matthew Purdy, "Wave of New Laws Seeks to Confine Sex Offenders," *The New York Times*, June 29, 1997. Reprinted with permission from *The New
York Times*.

A Wave of New Laws

Commitment laws are being used particularly aggressively in New Jersey, where Megan Kanka was killed. There, an average of more than one sex offender a month is involuntarily sent to a mental hospital as prosecutors take advantage of the state's expanded definition of mental illness. And in Wisconsin, the state has committed 82 convicted sex offenders to mental hospitals since its law was enacted in 1994.

Two days after the Supreme Court announced its ruling in the Kansas case, the New York State Legislature hurriedly passed its own version of the law and officials in several other states said they planned swift action to make it easier to forcibly hospitalize sex offenders who are deemed dangerous.

Sending offenders from prisons to hospitals is the clearest reflection yet of a perception that sex criminals are different from other criminals and require criminal justice mechanisms intended for them alone.

Driven by horrific sex crimes and a growing public angst, a law enforcement apparatus dedicated to sex offenders has been constructed around the country in just the last few years covering everything from longer sentences to enhanced parole supervision and many things beyond.

All states require released sex offenders to register their whereabouts. The Federal Government is requiring states to establish public notification programs. DNA databanks collect samples from sex offenders and, in some cases, other felons. In California and Montana, officials have approved using hormones to reduce sex drives of repeat offenders. "Enticement laws" in many states make it a crime to lure children for an illicit purpose.

"We're grasping at what to do with these people," said Carla Stovall, the Attorney General in Kansas. "Because of the harm that they pose, we need to have different methods for dealing with them because they are so different from bank robbers."

Even as advocates for tough restrictions on sex offenders celebrate the Supreme Court's decision, new measures are under discussion. On June 27, 1997, the National Center for Missing and Exploited Children, a prime force behind the passage of sex offender laws nationwide, convened the Sex Offender Strategy Summit in Washington to discuss its recommendations for state officials. On the list for consideration were measures like chemical castration and trained teams of "cybercops" to combat "sexual exploitation, pornography and enticement" on the Internet.

Against this wave, lawyers for convicted sex criminals and some doctors who treat them have warned against hysteria, questioning the perception of sex offenders as a monolithic group of dangerous recidivists for whom there is no treatment.

"Politically, it is easily the slowest moving target in the political spectrum," said John S. Furlong, a former sex crimes prosecutor in Trenton who now represents convicted sex offenders trying to fight commitment actions.

Fred Berlin, a psychiatrist who founded the Johns Hopkins Sexual Disorders Clinic in Baltimore, said treatment is often effective in reducing the proclivities of sex offenders. He said that a 1991 study of 600 men treated at his clinic found that about 8 percent repeated their crimes after five years. A study released in February 1997 by the Federal Bureau of Justice Statistics found that three years after being released from prison, about 41 percent of all violent offenders had been arrested for new felonies, while 19.5 percent of rapists had been arrested for a new crime.

"The notion that these are the most dangerous people in the community and the most likely to repeat needs to be looked at a lot more dispassionately," Dr. Berlin said.

But the passion for new laws runs high, especially since law enforcement officials report that two-thirds of those serving prison terms for sexual assault had children or teenagers as victims.

The Justice Department reports that the number of prisoners serving time for violent sexual assault has increased by 15 percent a year between 1980 and 1997, twice the average growth rate of the prison population as a whole.

A Response to Horrific Crimes

In state after state, attention has been focused on sexual offenders who have committed horrific crimes.

There was a 7-year-old boy in Washington State who was raped, stabbed and castrated by a repeat sex offender in May 1989—a case that gave rise to the nation's first civil commitment law for sex offenders. There was Megan Kanka, whose 1994 rape and murder at the hands of a convicted pedophile, Jesse K. Timmendequas, set off sex offender registration and community notification laws around the country. In 1993, there was 20-year-old Stephanie Schmidt of Pittsburg, Kan., who was murdered by a paroled rapist, which led to the law that was upheld by the Supreme Court in June 1997.

"I think the entire country has been moved by the tragedy of these cases," said Peter Verniero, the Attorney General for New Jersey. "These are highly honorable and noble principles behind these statutes, to protect children and those most vulnerable in our society."

Local outrage turned into a nationwide movement through a belief that the criminal justice system could not deal with sex offenders driven by inner demons that are impervious to punishment and deterrence.

"One of the points we've made from the beginning is that sex offenders are different," said Ernie Allen, the president of the National Center for Missing and Exploited Children. "Because of the nature of these offenses, because of the psychological element in their offense, because of the high risk of reoffending, because of the population they prey on, the government has an obligation to do more than say, 'Do your time and go forth and sin no more.'"

Civil Commitment Laws

The most far-reaching of the measures are the civil commitment laws, which, in addition to Kansas, Washington State, New Jersey and Wisconsin, are also in place in Arizona, California and Minnesota.

In general, the laws allow for a sex offender to be committed to a mental hospital if a court finds the person has a "mental abnormality" or a "personality disorder" and is likely to commit sexual violence. Commitments in most states are usually reviewed by courts at least once a year to determine if they should continue.

"As a society, you are faced with dangerous recidivists who are not normal, by any measure, but they are not insane, as the law defines insane," said Sarah Sappington, an assistant attorney general in Washington State, who wrote a brief on behalf of 38 states in support of the Kansas law in the Supreme Court.

Opponents of the laws assert that the measures dispose of the usual definition of mental illness merely to extend the incarceration of feared convicts.

The Kansas case involved Leroy Hendricks, who acknowledged abusing and molesting children since 1955, and said that he would only stop abusing children when he died. He challenged his 1994 commitment to a special secure mental hospital as soon as his prison term ended.

In a 5-to-4 decision, the Court said that state legislators were free to include mental abnormalities like pedophilia in a definition of mental illness and that civil commitment can follow a prison sentence without amounting to double punishment for one crime. In his dissent, Justice Stephen G. Breyer said that while the state committed Mr. Hendricks to treat him, there was evidence that he was not being treated. Therefore, the commitment "begins to look punitive." Kansas officials say committed sex offenders are now receiving treatment.

Eric Janus, a professor at William Mitchell College of Law in St. Paul, Minn., who has challenged Minnesota's civil commitment law, said the new laws are reminiscent of "sexual psychopath" laws in many states earlier in the twentieth century. "The early laws were applied at exhibitionists, consenting homosexuals, nonviolent pedophiles— people who were seen at the time as deviant and unpleasant to have around," he said.

But unlike the earlier laws, which were intended as an alternative to prisons, the new laws amount to "additional penal incarceration for people whose initial sentence the public now regrets as too short," Professor Janus said.

Even with the court having settled the commitment issue, the debate is likely to continue.

"We have not decided to incarcerate them for life or kill them," said Kay Jackson, a psychologist who treats paroled sex offenders in New York City. "We have a big social dilemma about what to do with these people."

Cyber-Rape: Responding to Online Sexual Violence

Debra Michals

Freelance writer Debra Michals discusses a relatively new phenomenon in the following selection: graphic sexual violence in the
realm of cyberspace. In "chat rooms" and other interactive spaces,
female Internet users can inadvertently encounter brutal sexual
fantasies depicting gang rape, sadism, and incest, Michals writes.
Although "cyber-rape" cannot be equated with physical rape, she
notes, some women have reported being emotionally traumatized
by sexual brutality online. Moreover, the author points out, there
have been cases in which unbalanced individuals carried out their
violent online fantasies in the real world. To counter the potential
dangers of online sexual violence, Michals maintains that women
should be assertive on the internet and refuse to let sexual bullies
get away with being abusive in cyberspace.

On a summer night in 1995 I witnessed my first gang rape. I stumbled
across it while exploring America Online's (AOL) "chat rooms" (areas
in which Internet users converse with each other on specific subjects
in real time). Having heard so much about the potential for human
interaction in this burgeoning communications medium known as
cyberspace, I decided to check it out. That's when I began my noctur-
nal forays on AOL. In my initial searches, I discovered that there was
lots of chatter, lots of flirting, and lots of sex—most of it banal reflec-
tions of barroom culture. Then, one night, as I scrolled through the
list of rooms, among those created by individual members rather than
AOL, I saw one titled "Rape Fantasy." Couldn't be, I said to myself,
but finally decided that I had to know. So I called it up on-screen and,
to my shock, entered a room where a gang rape was taking place.
There, on my screen, five men were writing about brutally violating a
woman who seemed to be encouraging them.

A "Cyber-Rape"

Here's what appeared on my screen (although the names of the participants have been changed, they closely parallel the ones they

Reprinted from Debra Michals, "Cyber-Rape: How Virtual Is It?" *Ms.*, March/April
1997. Copyright © 1997 *Ms.* Magazine. Reprinted with permission from *Ms.*

used online):
Greg0987: Hold her down, guys.
Panther: I got her legs.
Robodude: I got her pinned.
Greg0987: She wants it bad. Don't ya, bitch?
Brenda: Give it to me. Give it to me good.
Panther: I'll fuck you so hard, it'll tear you open.
Bigcock: Like it rough, stupid cunt? Hit her in the face, Greg. Smash her.
Pussyeater: Don't move or I'll cut you with this knife.
Greg0987: Me first, then the rest of you go. Stop moving or I'll hit you, bitch.

Barely a minute passed—though it felt like hours—before I broke my silence.
Me: What the hell is going on in here?
Greg0987: We're raping her, what do you think?
Me: I think this is really sick.
Greg0987: Chill out. We're just playing.
Me: Playing? Women are raped and beaten every day, and it isn't play.
Greg0987: If you don't like it, get out of here. You don't have to stay.

Before I could respond, I was assaulted by so many private messages telling me to shut up or get lost that my machine jammed and I had to reboot. I sat there in front of my computer, feeling shocked and enraged.

Was this some unusual occurrence? Hardly. After the skirmish over the passage of the Communications Decency Act in 1995, many of these overtly violent spaces seemed to have disappeared from the AOL chat room roster. But their disappearance is an illusion. Although AOL no longer allows words like "rape" or "sex" to be used in naming public spaces, anything goes when it comes to user-created private rooms, and Internet users also skirt the ban by coming up with inventive names. The result is that anyone seeking a "gang bang," or a host of other sexually graphic and often violent scenarios, including "incest," can either find it easily online, or create their own room.

It hardly takes a rocket scientist to guess what may be going on in rooms with titles like "daughterblowsdad," "UnusualDesires," and "Torture Females." When I checked out "Torture Females" in October 1996, a man threatened to burn my hand and hang a 19-pound weight from the inside of my vagina with sharp pins. All this to get him hard. And in one incest room, on more than one occasion, participants who claimed to be teenage boys described acts of sexual violence against female siblings that seemed all too real. But my experiences on AOL were pretty tame compared to what goes on in unsupervised Internet Relay Chats, MUDs (multiuser dimensions/dungeons), or similar interactive spaces that have few boundaries or controls imposed by any online service.

The often violent nature of many of the sexual "fantasies" played out in these interactive chat rooms raises important questions about the dark side of human sexuality and the way in which the Internet permits its free and unquestioned expression in easily accessible public spaces. Despite the disclaimers of many of the participants that what occurs on the Net is pure fantasy, questions abound. If "words *are* deeds," as Sherry Turkle, a sociology of science professor at the Massachusetts Institute of Technology, notes in her book *Life on the Screen: Identity in the Age of the Internet*, what exactly are the deeds being carried out in these spaces? Do they belong merely to the realm of fantasy role-play or do they transform the sexual psyches of the participants? Are fantasies being explored or are past deeds being recounted? Do these games ultimately blur the distinction between fantasy and the reality of women's sexual desires? Or, since men are so often at the helm of these games, do they merely reinscribe male domination of female sexuality in both realms—the real and the imagined? While participants will tell you they understand the difference between fantasy and reality, what of the lurker who never participates but avidly takes it all in? How can we measure the impact on him or on the woman who consents to an erotic scenario and finds it spiraling out of control?

Given the number of actual rapes that are committed in our society, this online behavior obviously mimics real life. But what effect does it have on us in both our real and virtual lives? Clearly, "virtual rape" is not the same as the rape a woman experiences in the physical world. But something as yet unnameable is going on in chat rooms where an erotic scenario can shift to a gang bang with a few keystrokes from an observing male who jumps in with, "Let's skull-fuck the bitch." It is not that all, or even most, Internet sex is violent; rather, that the potential for violent intrusions hovers around any exchange, be it sexual or not.

Troubling Internet Experiences

Women on the receiving end of this graphic sexual violence on the Net have indeed reported being traumatized by the experience. While many may turn off their computers or leave a chat area if they feel attacked, they often have trouble shaking the memory that a stranger at a far-off computer terminal wanted to hurt them. Vonnie Cesar, a 27-year-old nurse and regular Internet user from Albany, Georgia, is still troubled by an early experience. "I went into a chat room pretending to be a 15-year-old girl, just to see how people would respond to me," she explains. "One of the men asked me to go into a private room with him, and when I did, seven or eight other guys came in and started sending me pictures of women who had been beaten and raped. The pictures looked real—not like some studio shot or makeup job. They said they wanted to rape me, spank me until I bled. What made it especially scary is that, as far as they knew, I was just a young girl, a virgin in fact."

Cesar's story has disturbing implications. What if she had actually been a 15-year-old girl? Or what if one of the male participants, some of whom may be teenagers themselves, decided to act his sick fantasies out on a real girl? While most Internet providers allow parents to restrict children's access to sexually explicit areas online, the reality is that not all parents become so involved. Consequently, there are many young people frequenting Internet chat rooms and being influenced by what they encounter. For young people still learning the difference between fantasy and reality, the lessons may well be that violence is a normal part of male behavior, that for men sexual domination is erotic, and that for women passivity and a willingness to be victimized are the rule.

Because the Internet is still fairly new, it remains to be seen how such violent role-playing will affect our sexual relationships and our larger goals of ensuring male respect for women. "The question is, are we desensitizing people about how they can relate to each other, rather than helping them move toward more compassionate relationships?" asks Patti Britton, Ph.D., a clinical sexologist and a spokeswoman for Feminists for Free Expression, an anti-censorship group. Regardless of the risks, Britton remains opposed to stifling free speech. "I don't think we can draw a causal link at this point, but what I do know is that what we suppress, expresses. If we keep our fantasies in darkness, they grow stronger. So maybe we'll find that through the Internet, we're 'Gestalting' out the demons that keep us from having healthy relationships." Perhaps. But isn't it more likely that airing such violent inclinations freely and without reproach will merely normalize these tendencies, inuring society to the viciousness and inequality at its core.

No doubt, the Internet makes it easier for disturbed people to find each other or to identify unwitting victims. Participants' risk of being victimized is heightened by the fact that the Internet also encourages a false sense of trust and of what's real and what's make-believe. There is no eye contact in cyberspace, no opportunity to hear the inflection in a person's voice. A person can omit certain facts about themselves, or accentuate the qualities that might be more socially acceptable—so even the most unbalanced person might appear sane online.

A Link Between Fantasy and Reality

Two cases in 1996 seem to indicate that for some Internet users, there is a dangerous link between online fantasy and real-world behavior. In October 1996, a Maryland woman was found murdered in a shallow grave behind the home of a man she had met on the Internet, to whom she had allegedly expressed a desire to be sexually tortured and killed. Slightly more than a month later, a 20-year-old student at Barnard College in New York City claimed that she had been held captive and sexually assaulted by a Columbia University graduate student she had met on the Internet and agreed to meet in real life.

While one of the grad student's attorneys has cited the woman's sexually graphic e-mail to him in claiming that he "didn't force anybody
to do anything," the case points up the essential dilemma about
where or whether fantasy and reality intersect. If, as many users
assert, what is said online should be taken as fantasy, then the young
woman's explicit e-mail should not be taken as evidence of her real-
life desires. Or should it?

Given that more and more women are going online, the prevalence of graphic depictions of sexual violence will bring pornography
into an increasing number of women's lives. "Up to now, pornography has been somewhat avoidable," says Gloria Steinem. "You can't
avoid the newsstands, but you don't have to open the magazines."
Steinem sees some slight benefit to this. "Now, the Internet brings it
into your home, and there's the chance for an important education
for people who think it's rare or harmless, or who don't realize how
sadistic pornography really is." A woman seeking anything from an
erotic online encounter to professional networking could find herself
being accosted by some Internet junkie seeking to impose his twisted
fantasies. Women in offices also report that pornographic images and
fantasies are becoming an increasingly common workplace reality, as
male coworkers gather around each other's computer terminals to
check out sex sites online.

As of August 1996, there were approximately 36 million Internet
users, a figure that is growing rapidly, according to Nielsen Media
Research, a polling and tracking group. But although more women are
online today than a few years ago, most estimates still hold the ratio
of males to females at two to one. For the moment, some of the most
flagrant forms of male domination seem to flourish on the Internet
because men, by sheer force of their numbers, dictate the tone and
content of what occurs. Perhaps the pervasiveness of violent role-
playing online is a reflection of male angst in an era of changing gender norms. Perhaps virtual rapists represent patriarchy's storm troops,
who hope to hold the forces of history at bay by engaging in this last
stand on the edge of a new frontier. If this is the case, sexual violence
online may function as both an assertion of dominance and a means
of chasing women away from the Internet. The experience of Susan
Racer, a student at New York University, who reports being accosted
upon entering some chat rooms by messages such as "I've just
smacked you, and you're lying on the floor" is an all too familiar one.
It's as if she is being immediately reminded of her place in the virtual
world before she has a chance to assert herself there.

Role Playing on the Internet

That many Internet providers guarantee users anonymity adds to the
sense of license. People can choose screen names that disguise their
identities and gender. Providers also allow users to create a profile of

themselves—a brief and publicly accessible résumé indicating age, sex, hobbies, and hometown—at their own discretion. Some users never submit any information, others stay close to the truth, and still others choose to alter their profiles to reflect whatever role or identity they wish to take on.

While anonymity makes sense in online support groups for survivors of abuse or incest, it also enables would-be aggressors to act without repercussions. "People experiment online with identities and actions they would never actually adopt in real life," says Claudia Springer, an English and film studies professor at Rhode Island College and author of *Electronic Eros: Bodies and Desire in the Post-industrial Age*. "The Internet offers an opportunity to be radically other than oneself without suffering the consequences."

Disguising one's gender can provide some protection from online abuse. Nikki Douglas, the editor of the Web 'zine *RiotGrrl*, says she sometimes goes online posing as a man to avoid the harassing messages and rape photos she receives when she signs on as herself. But gender cloaking can also take a number of bizarre turns. Consider, for example, that "Brenda," the woman being gang-raped in the chat room I entered, may have been a man posing as a woman. In such cases, these female impersonators are representing their fiction of what women want as though it were the real thing. "If men are playing the role of the rape victim, they are playing out their fantasies of women responding to rape so they can have this text out there," says Catharine MacKinnon, law professor at the University of Michigan and coauthor, with Andrea Dworkin, of proposed civil rights ordinances recognizing pornography as sex discrimination. "It normalizes the violence for them by making it seem as if the woman likes it."

Defining Control and Consent

Certainly some women do consent not only to cybersex but also to violent scenarios. In fact, many techno-feminists argue that this medium represents a kind of sexual revolution for women in which they can act out their wildest desires with complete safety. Women who enjoy cybersex say it has enabled them to explore their sexual fantasies; they can go online and engage in an evening of anonymous sex without the fear they would experience from a similar scene in real life. But as in the case of that Barnard student, the world is not so tidy. Users often forget that across the miles, at another computer, is a real person who may not be trustworthy or emotionally balanced.

Because women can log off whenever things get too violent, Carla Sinclair, author of *Net Chick: A Smart Girl Guide to the Wired World*, denies that women can be sexually violated online. "You're not going to get on the Internet and end up attacked in some dark alley," says Sinclair, who posed for the April 1996 "Women of the Internet" spread in *Playboy*. "All this talk perpetuates the idea that women are weak and that they have to be protected. You're only a victim if you say you are. You can empower yourself by getting out of a chat room when it gets uncomfortable. People have a right to choose where they go, just as they need to take responsibility for the consequences their choices produce."

The problem with the way babe feminists like Sinclair define control and consent is that these words become synonymous with female compliance or retreat. Women either play the game or leave, which is hardly empowering. "In some cases, turning off the machine is a cop-out and could be damaging to a woman's perception of herself and her sense of control," argues Laurel Gilbert, coauthor of *SurferGrrrls*, a women's guide to the Internet. "It could be analogous to the ways in which women shut down after being sexually abused and are left feeling awful about themselves and what happened to them."

But notions of power or freedom are at best an illusion in cases of online violence in which women are submitting to their own violation. Regardless of how "powerful" they may feel, they are still following a patriarchal cultural script that reaffirms gender hierarchy and validates the assumption that *all* women really want to be treated this way. "I would not call it a feminist triumph because we can choose to have our lovers beat us silly in this or any realm," says Elizabeth Reba Weise, coeditor of *Wired Women: Gender and New Realities in Cyber-space*. However, "I would draw the distinction between cheerfully play-acting with your partner and having someone sew your labia shut. Having your partner call you a slut or a whore online hardly subverts the patriarchal order."

Worse, as MacKinnon argues, is that the consequences of these games may extend beyond the individual woman herself. "The word 'consent' can cover up some very important issues. If it's truly a woman being violated, seeming to go along with it, we don't know if she was sexually abused as a child and is therefore feeling this form of assault as being loved. We do know that most women used in pornography were sexually abused as children. But a lot of other women stand to be harmed by her appearing to welcome abuse. Whatever her experience, she isn't the only woman in the world. As all these men enjoy her purported consent to being violated, she gives sexual credibility to a male fantasy that can get other women hurt."

Reshaping Online Interactions

What does all this bode for the future? There have already been cases where sexual violence online has reached beyond the keyboard. It seems inevitable that more such cases will occur. And there is no doubt that new technology will also reshape online interactions. New sites under the CUSeeMe banner have sprung up on the World Wide Web, where users employ standard video cameras to watch each other act out fantasies in real time. According to Donna Hoffman, associate professor of management at Vanderbilt University in Nashville, video-conferencing of this nature, though offering only slow and grainy pictures at present, will likely become more refined in the next few years. In addition to the plethora of interactive CD-ROM sex games available, experts also expect we'll be seeing sensory devices that let users feel what they envision. Bill LeFurgy, editor of the weekly newsletter "Culture in Cyberspace," predicts that "in five to ten years it will probably be possible for people to hook up sensory devices to themselves that let them feel as they would if they were actually doing what they imagine online."

Meanwhile, women are starting to assert themselves online, and a new generation of Internet feminists is emerging with full claims on cyberspace. Some women are posting erotica on the Web, and others are standing up to those who, with violent messages, try to chase them out of chat rooms. One woman has launched her own campaign to seize control of sexually violent chat rooms and turn them into loving spaces. She claims that "this medium has tremendous potential to teach, and I want these guys to learn how they should treat the women in their lives when it comes to sex."

The shortage of women online may give women who choose to engage these men in their playpens more control, since many of them seem willing to consent to any scenario just to have cybersex with a real woman. And some women do see this as an opportunity to assert themselves by creating a woman-friendly climate that provides a more accurate representation of women's sexuality and humanity. Techno-feminists like Douglas and Weise argue that, rather than fleeing violent spaces, women should turn the tables and hold their ground.

But many of us have no desire to engage the sexually violent Internet user or to play sex games online. So what do we do when they invade our turf? Groups of women together can chase violators out of chat rooms by simply barraging the interloper with "get lost" messages. We can also insist that Internet providers prevent users from changing their online names and profiles at will. While users could remain anonymous, by making them stick to one name, a degree of accountability would be instituted. You wouldn't be able to behave abusively under one name and then take another one to hide behind. Some providers, like The WELL, a small California-based bulletin board, already employ this policy, and users report few problems with sexual violence.

With computers and the Internet becoming an increasing presence in the lives of children, it is important to educate them early about the prevalence of sexual violence online, and about the difference between fantasy and reality. Children should come to the Internet knowing that what exists in the recesses of people's imaginations is not necessarily the truth about what they as individuals, or what women and men collectively, may want to experience in real life.

Young people should know what kind of people may lurk online, and be warned not to trust everyone they meet, not to give out personal information, and not to yield their right to this space to cyberspace bullies, or anyone else who tries to manipulate them.

If there's a moral to all this, it's don't just sit back and take the abuse. The most powerful thing women can do is refuse to collaborate.

ORGANIZATIONS TO CONTACT

The editors have compiled the following list of organizations concerned with the issues presented in this book. The descriptions are derived from materials provided by the organizations. All have publications or information available for interested readers. The list was compiled on the date of publication of the present volume; the information provided here may change. Be aware that many organizations take several weeks or longer to respond to inquiries, so allow as much time as possible.

Center for the Prevention of Sexual and Domestic Violence (CPSDV)
936 N. 34th St., Suite 200, Seattle, WA 98013
(206) 634-1903 • fax: (206) 634-0115
e-mail: cpsdv@cpsdv.org • website: www.cpsdv.org

The center is an interreligious ministry addressing issues of sexual and domestic violence. Its goal is to engage religious leaders in the task of ending abuse through institutional and social change. The center publishes educational videos, the quarterly newsletter *Working Together,* and many books, including *Violence Against Women and Children: A Christian Theological Sourcebook* and *Sexual Violence: The Unmentionable Sin—An Ethical and Pastoral Perspective.*

Center for Women Policy Studies (CWPS)
1211 Connecticut Ave. NW, Suite 312, Washington, DC 20036
(202) 872-1770 • fax: (202) 296-8962
e-mail: cwpsx@aol.com

Established in 1972, the CWPS is an independent feminist policy research and advocacy institution. The center studies policies affecting the social, legal, health, and economic status of women. It publishes the booklets *Campus Gang Rape* and *Campus Sexual Harassment,* as well as reports on a variety of topics related to women's equality and empowerment, including sexual harassment, campus rape, and violence against women.

Family Violence and Sexual Assault Institute (FVSAI)
1310 Clinic Dr., Tyler, TX 75701
(903) 595-6600
website: http://ericps.ed.vivc.edu/npin/reswork/workorgs/fvsainst.html

The FVSAI networks among people and agencies involved in studying, treating, protecting, or otherwise dealing with violent or abusive families. The FVSAI maintains a computerized database that includes unpublished or hard-to-find articles and papers, which are available for copying and postage charges. Publications include the bibliography *Sexual Abuse/Incest Survivors* and the quarterly *Family Violence and Sexual Assault Bulletin.*

National Association of College and University Attorneys
1 Dupont Circle, Suite 620, Washington, DC 20036
(202) 833-8390 • fax: (202) 296-8379
e-mail: nacua@nacua.org • website: www.nacua.org

The association represents approximately fourteen hundred U.S. and Canadian colleges and universities in legal matters. It compiles and distributes legal decisions, opinions, and other writings and information on legal problems affecting colleges and universities. Publications include *Acquaintance Rape on Campus: A Model for Institutional Response* and *Crime on Campus*.

National Coalition of Free Men
PO Box 129, Manhasset, NY 11030
(516) 482-6378
e-mail: ncfm@liii.com • website: www.ncfm.org

The coalition's members include men seeking "a fair and balanced perspective on gender issues." The organization promotes men's legal rights in issues such as false accusation of rape, sexual harassment, and sexual abuse. It conducts research, sponsors educational programs, maintains a database on men's issues, and publishes the bimonthly *Transitions*.

National Criminal Justice Reference Service (NCJRS)
PO Box 6000, Rockville, MD 20849-6000
(310) 519-5063
e-mail: askncjrs@ncjrs.org • website: www.ncjrs.org

In 1972, the National Institute of Justice—the research and development agency of the U.S. Department of Justice—established the NCJRS as its clearinghouse. The NCJRS provides studies and statistics on child rape victims, child victimizers, and violence against women. Among its publications are the reports "The Criminal Justice and Community Response to Rape" and "When the Victim Is a Child."

Office for Victims of Crime Resource Center
810 Seventh St. NW, Washington, DC 20531
(800) 627-6872
website: www.ojp.usdoj.gov/ovc

Established in 1983 by the U.S. Department of Justice, the resource center is a primary source of information regarding victim-related issues. It answers questions by using national and regional statistics, research findings, and a network of victim advocates and organizations. The center distributes all Office of Justice Programs publications, including *Female Victims of Violent Crime* and *Sexual Assault: An Overview*.

People Against Rape (PAR)
PO Box 5876, Naperville, IL 60567
(800) 877-7252
e-mail: Personal_Empowerment_Programs@msn.com

People Against Rape primarily seeks to help teens and children avoid becoming the victims of sexual assault and rape by providing instruction in the basic principles of self-defense. PAR further promotes self-esteem and motivation of teens and college students through educational programs. Publications include the books *Defend: Preventing Date Rape and Other Sexual Assaults* and *Sexual Assault: How to Defend Yourself*.

Sex Information and Education Council of the U.S. (SIECUS)
130 W. 42nd St., Suite 350, New York, NY 10036-7802
(212) 819-9770 • fax: (212) 819-9776
e-mail: siecus@siecus.org • website: www.siecus.org

SIECUS is a clearinghouse for information on sexuality, with a special interest in sex education. It publishes sex education curricula, the bimonthly newsletter *SIECUS Report*, and fact sheets on sex education issues. Its articles, bibliographies, and book reviews often address the role of sex education in identifying, reducing, and preventing sexual violence.

Survivor Connections
52 Lyndon Rd., Cranston, RI 02905-1121
(401) 941-2548

Survivor Connections is an activist organization for survivors of sexual assault. It provides referrals to attorneys, therapists, and peer support groups. The organization also seeks to educate the public about legislation affecting survivors and encourages criminal prosecution and civil claims against perpetrators. A quarterly newspaper, the *Survivor Activist*, is available to the general public.

BIBLIOGRAPHY

Books

Beverly Allen   *Rape Warfare: The Hidden Genocide in Bosnia-Herzegovina and Croatia*. Minneapolis: University of Minnesota Press, 1996.

Julie A. Allison and Lawrence S. Wrightsman   *Rape: The Misunderstood Crime*. Newbury Park, CA: Sage, 1993.

Helen Benedict   *Recovery: How to Survive Sexual Assault for Women, Men, Teenagers, Their Friends and Families*. New York: Columbia University Press, 1994.

Jeffrey R. Benedict   *Athletes and Acquaintance Rape*. Thousand Oaks, CA: Sage, 1998.

Raquel Kennedy Bergen   *Wife Rape: Understanding the Response of Survivors and Service Providers*. Thousand Oaks, CA: Sage, 1996.

Susan Brownmiller   *Against Our Will: Men, Women, and Rape*. New York: Simon and Schuster, 1975.

Emilie Buchwald, Pamela Fletcher, and Martha Roth, eds.   *Transforming a Rape Culture*. Minneapolis: Milkweed Editions, 1993.

David M. Buss and Neil. M. Malamuth   *Sex, Power, Conflict: Evolutionary and Feminist Perspectives*. New York: Oxford University Press, 1996.

Nancy A. Crowell and Ann W. Burgess, eds.   *Understanding Violence Against Women*, Washington, DC: National Academy Press, 1996.

Lisa M. Cuklanz   *Rape on Prime Time: Television, Masculinity, and Sexual Violence*. Philadelphia: University of Pennsylvania Press, 2000.

Rus Ervin Funk   *Stopping Rape: A Challenge for Men*. Philadelphia: New Society Publishers, 1995.

December Green   *Gender Violence in Africa: African Women's Responses*. New York: St. Martin's, 1999.

Jeanne Gregory   *Policing Sexual Assault*. New York: Routledge, 1999.

Gordon C. Nagayama Hall   *Theory-Based Assessment, Treatment, and Prevention of Sexual Aggression*. New York: Oxford University Press, 1996.

Mary P. Koss et al.   *No Safe Haven: Male Violence Against Women at Home, at Work, and in the Community*. Washington, DC: American Psychological Association, 1994.

Mary E. Odem and Judy Clay-Warner, eds.   *Confronting Rape and Sexual Assault*. Wilmington, DE.: Scholarly Resources, 1998.

Katie Roiphe   *The Morning After: Sex, Fear, and Feminism on Campus*. New York: Little, Brown, 1993.

Stephen J. Schulhofer	*Unwanted Sex: The Culture of Intimidation and the Failure of Law.* Cambridge, MA: Harvard University Press, 1998.
Martin D. Schwartz and Walter S. DeKeseredy	*Sexual Assault on the College Campus: The Role of Male Peer Support.* Thousand Oaks, CA: Sage, 1997.
Alice Sebold	*Lucky.* New York: Scribner, 1999.
Christina Hoff Somers	*Who Stole Feminism? How Women Have Betrayed Women.* New York: Simon & Schuster, 1994.
Adele M. Stan	*Debating Sexual Correctness: Pornography, Sexual Harassment, Date Rape, and the Politics of Sexual Equality.* New York: Dell, 1995.
Dennis J. Stevens	*Inside the Mind of a Serial Rapist.* San Francisco: Austin & Winfield, 1999.
Andrew E. Taslitz	*Rape and the Culture of the Courtroom.* New York: New York University Press, 1999.
Randy Thornhill and Craig T. Palmer	*A Natural History of Rape: Biological Bases of Sexual Coercion.* Cambridge, MA: MIT Press, 2000.
Robin Warshaw	*I Never Called It Rape: The* Ms. *Report on Recognizing, Fighting, and Surviving Date and Acquaintance Rape.* New York: HarperPerennial, 1994.

Periodicals

Anonymous	"My Mentor, My Rapist," *Gentleman's Quarterly*, April 2000.
Jennifer Baumgardner	"What Does Rape Look Like?" *Nation*, January 3, 2000.
Alison Bell	"Date Rape," *Teen*, July 1997.
mimi bwouty	"Brenham's Paradise Lost," *Texas Monthly*, February 1997.
David R. Carlin	"Date Rape Fallacies: Can There Be Purely Voluntary Acts?" *Commonweal*, February 25, 1994.
Christopher D. Cook and Christian Parenti	"Rape Camp, USA," *In These Times*, December 27, 1998.
Meghan Daum	"Coming Down Hard: Abuse of Rohypnol," *Gentlemen's Quarterly*, September 1997.
Sam Dillon	"Rape and Murder Stalk Women in Northern Mexico," *New York Times*, April 19, 1998.
Ebony	"The Truth About Date Rape," September 1997.
Barbara Ehrenreich	"How 'Natural' Is Rape? Despite a Daffy New Theory, It's Not Just a Guy in Touch with His Inner Caveman," *Time*, January 31, 2000.
Amy Engeler	"'I Can't Hate This Baby,'" *Redbook*, February 1999.
Eric Felten	"Sex and the Single Soldier," *National Review*, April 7, 1997.
Josh Fischman	"A Fight over the Evolution of Rape," *U.S. News & World Report*, February 7, 2000.

Laura Flanders	"Rwanda's Living Casualties," *Ms.*, March/April 1998.
Alec Foege	"Silent No More," *People*, November 30, 1998.
Douglas Frantz	"On Cruise Ships, Silence Shrouds Crimes," *New York Times*, November 16, 1998.
Mary Gaitskill	"On Not Being a Victim," *Harper's*, March 1994.
Neil Gilbert	"Realities and Mythologies of Rape," *Society*, January/February 1998.
Sarah Glazer	"Punishing Sex Offenders," *CQ Researcher*, January 12, 1996. Available from 1414 22nd St. NW, Washington, DC 20037.
Neve Gordon	"Sanctioned Rape," *Humanist*, July/August 2000.
Linda Greenhouse	"Women Lose Right to Sue Attackers in Federal Court," *New York Times*, May 16, 2000.
Dick Haws	"The Elusive Numbers on False Rape," *Columbia Journalism Review*, November/December 1997.
Peter Hawthorne	"An Epidemic of Rapes," *Time*, November 1, 1999.
Bob Herbert	"How Many Innocent Prisoners?" *New York Times*, July 18, 1999.
Liz Holtzman and Alice Vachss	"Let's Get Tough on Rape," *On the Issues*, Summer 1994.
Ida M. Johnson and Robert T. Sigler	"Forced Sexual Intercourse on Campus: Crime or Offensive Behavior?" *Journal of Contemporary Criminal Justice*, vol. 12, no. 1, February 1996. Available from the Department of Criminal Justice, California State University, Long Beach, 1250 Bellflower Blvd., Long Beach, CA 90840.
Maura Kelly	"The Rape Stopper," *Glamour*, June 2000.
Richard Laliberte	"Victim to Rapist: 'It's Payback Time,'" *Redbook*, January 1999.
Donatella Lorch and Preston Mendenhall	"A War's Hidden Tragedy," *Newsweek*, August 14, 2000.
Mademoiselle	"How to Protect Yourself from Rape," November 1997.
Linda Marsa	"The New Date-Rape Drug," *Glamour*, November 1997.
Craig McCoy	"The Buried Rapes," *Columbia Journalism Review*, January/February 2000.
Judy Monroe	"Roofies: Horror Drug of the '90s," *Current Health*, 1997.
Debbie Morris with Gregg A. Lewis, ed.	"Dead Man Walking: The Victim Who Survived," *Ladies' Home Journal*, October 1998.
Ms.	"Peruvian Women Challenge an Ugly Rape Law," March/April 1997.
Maria Nadotti	"The Denim Defense," *Ms.*, June/July 1999.
New York Times	"When Rape Becomes Genocide," September 5, 1998.

Jane O'Hara	"Rape in the Military," *Maclean's*, May 25, 1998.
Valerie Oosterveld	"When Women Are the Spoils of War," *Unesco Courier*, July/August 1998.
Marjorie Preston	"She Lived a Nightmare," *Ladies' Home Journal*, November 1999.
Patrick Rogers	"Wake-Up," *People*, May 3, 1999.
Megan Rosenfeld	"The Male Animal: Two Scientists Explain Rape as a Natural Behavior and Cause an Unnatural Uproar," *Washington Post*, January 28, 2000. Available from Reprints, 1150 15th St. NW, Washington, DC, 20071.
Bruce Shapiro	"Rape's Defenders," *Nation*, July 1, 1996.
Nina Siegal	"Stopping Abuse in Prison," *Progressive*, April 1999.
Alessandra Stanley	"Ruling on Tight Jeans and Rape Sets Off Anger in Italy," *New York Times*, February 16, 1999.
Kelly Starling	"Black Women and Rape," *Ebony*, November 1998.
Del Thiessen and Robert K. Young	"Investigating Sexual Coercion," *Society*, March/April 1994.
Sheila Weller	"The Making of a Serial Rapist," *New York*, November 3, 1997.
Kevin Whitelaw	"Rape as a War Crime," *U.S. News & World Report*, April 3, 2000.

INDEX